2.90 ¹²⁄₆₈

Pat·T. Liebenberg.

ON TREK AGAIN

On Trek Again

An account of the Rugby tour in Southern Africa
by the 1968 Lions

J. B. G. THOMAS

PELHAM BOOKS

First published in Great Britain by
PELHAM BOOKS LTD
26 *Bloomsbury Street*
London, W.C.1
1968

© 1968 *by J. B. G. Thomas*

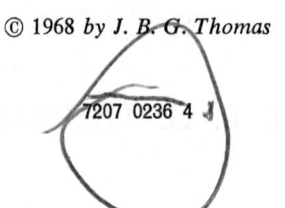

7207 0236 4

Set and printed in Great Britain by
Tonbridge Printers Ltd, Peach Hall Works, Tonbridge, Kent
in Times ten on twelve point, and bound by
James Burn at Esher, Surrey

To the Group
and my Welsh colleagues on tour
—the Fizzers

CONTENTS

Preface 13

ILLUSTRATIONS

ACKNOWLEDGEMENTS

The author's grateful thanks are due to the following for their help in obtaining the photographs reproduced in this book: *Cape Times:* 1, 2, 3, 31, 34, 35; *Rhodesia Herald:* 4, 5; *J. Wilkinson:* 7, 8; *Sunday Express, Jo'burg:* 9; *Associated Press:* 10, 15, 16; *Star, Jo'burg:* 11, 12; *Evening Post, Port Elizabeth:* 13; *Cape Argus:* 14, 17; *Die Burger, Cape Town:* 18, 19, 20, 21, 25, 26; *Sunday Times, Jo'burg:* 22, 23, 24; *G. G. R. Hofmeister, Jo'burg:* 33, 37.

PREFACE

The 1968 Lions were not the most successful side ever to leave the shores of the British Isles, but they did much better than many critics anticipated. Had the Third Test been won, the Lions would have been fêted, but because no test was won, their fine provincial record has been overlooked.

In this book I have attempted to record their journey through Southern Africa; the matches played, the people met and the outstanding incidents on and off the field. For me it was a happy tour, as I am sure it was for the Lions themselves, and their camp followers.

I would like to thank Thomson Provincial Newspapers, and especially the *Western Mail*, who sent me on my fifth successive Lions tour. My thanks also are due to the Four Home Unions, the South African Board, and all the kind people who helped so much on tour, but especially the Group; my three close friends, Vivian, Cliff and Dewi; the South African Newspapers and their staffs, and especially the Argus Group, and last but not least the Lions themselves, who made the writing of this book possible.

J. B. G. Thomas
Cardiff, August 1968

PART ONE

The Tour in Retrospect

CHAPTER ONE

The Judgment

It may never be possible to assess the true value of Tom Kiernan's 1968 British Lions, for they failed in the test series, lost three nil with one match drawn, but succeeded in the provincial matches, losing only one of sixteen played. They could have been better than they were and enjoyed a happier record in the tests. However, when one assesses the strength and weaknesses of the side, one must say that it did as well as could be expected. At the end of the 1967–68 season in the British Isles, rugby standards were not high in any of the four home countries, and while the touring party was near enough to being the best that could be selected, it was never regarded as a world-beating unit.

Therefore one could argue that in fact the team did better than was expected before it flew out of London Airport on May 12, and even developed into a side that could have won a test match as well as sharing one. It wasted chances at test level and was plagued throughout the tour by injuries to key players. Three replacements were provided in a twenty-match tour, the same number as in 1959 on a thirty-three match tour.

The record of the 1968 side compares favourably with that of the 1962 side in Southern Africa, and thus the Lions did not deteriorate on this tour as did the 1966 side in Australia and New Zealand after the unlucky 1959 tour. Thus, one is prepared to say that the 1968 and 1962 sides had a great deal in common, apart from their record, which is equal in the tests. They developed good packs of forwards, but never played well enough behind, and it was because of a lack of generalship and control, and inaccuracy, that prevented the backs from establishing themselves. It is a well-known fact that to succeed in South Africa one has to win the ball and then use it, and not since 1955 has this been done.

The conditions there favour strong, fast and elusive running, but the 1968 Lions could not supply this, for they carried the

basic weaknesses of British Rugby deep into the Southern Hemisphere, the aimless kick ahead. It was tragic to watch this in
match after match, and particularly the tests, until the ploy
appeared the only progressive tactic known to the Lions. It is
true that Thompson's men of 1955 and Dawson's men of 1959,
had brilliant backs, for the 1950's were the best post-war years
in British Rugby. Morgan, Baker, Risman and company were
pivots that could control and they had centres with them to exploit
the half-gap. Most of their play was positive, which is in striking
contrast to the 1968 side.

Yet the team's weakness was a basic one in British Rugby, and
hard though Dawson may have coached them – and he did a good
job with the forwards – he did not succeed in eradicating the basic
weaknesses of back play or inspiring them to run with the ball
and keep the wings in play. Being a wing in a modern Lions
side, as indeed in any of the national XV's in the British Isles, is
a boring job, for it consists of just three phases of play; throwing
in from touch, chasing kicks ahead and covering diagonal kicks
in defence.

They are the forgotten men of attacking rugby, and as long as
we continue to forget them at home, our play overseas will never
improve. Wings can be used to stretch defences and for switches
in attack. Let them do the kicking-on; see that they get the ball
with space in which to move, but do not let them fade completely
from the game. This time the leading try scorers reached six and
no more, while O'Reilly on a 25 match tour in 1955 got sixteen.
Yet the 1968 side scored 377 points in 20 matches as compared
with Smith's side's total of 401 in 25 matches, and 457 in 25
matches by the 1955 side. It scored 55 tries to 94 by the 1955
side, and but for the excellent kicking of Kiernan and Hiller, the
scoring figures would have been much reduced. It is sad to think
that while having two such fine place kickers, the 1968 Lions did
not score enough tries.

One may well ask . . . where did the 1968 Lions fail, following
such a tremendous build-up and preparation? Since the end of the
tour many answers have been supplied by those involved and on
the side-lines, and by folk at home who have followed the tour so
excellently portrayed on TV. Apart from the last test, in which a
touring side is generally on a hiding to nothing, the Lions held
their own and their one provincial defeat could have been

avoided had they taken their chances in the first half against the Transvaal.

The main weakness of the side was bad finishing and the inability of the backs to take their chances. They were not particularly creative as a group, and because of this needed to be much more basic and accurate in their play. The New Zealand All-Blacks of 1967 were not particularly creative behind the scrum, for they had four basic moves, but they were fast and accurate. The 1968 Lions never developed fast, accurate cohesion behind, and the injuries to key players had much to do with this.

Gibson was a disappointment at outside-half, for it was felt that South African conditions would see him blossom forth as a great player, but it was not so. He fell well behind Morgan, Baker, Risman, and even Waddell, as a tactical controller and feeder of the ball. It appeared as if he never had the confidence for the job or the vital judgment, to ensure that the service received from the forwards, sometimes good, sometimes bad, was used to the full. He never got his line swinging, and under Dawson's direction, the major offensive weapon appeared to be the long diagonal kick away from the forwards, in the hope that this would tire the opposition. Every time we saw this 'charade' enacted, Vivian Jenkins and myself winced, for the unemployed three-quarters must have been greatly inspired by it!

It may be wrong to criticise Gibson, for he may have been acting under 'orders' at all times, but he was not able to take charge of the situation in mid-field when there was need, such as in the second half of the Third Test at Cape Town. Much of the good work of the forwards was wasted by the wrong tactical approach behind.

Yet there were a few occasions when the backs rose to the occasion magnificently, especially in defence when the forwards were up against it. This was true of the Second Test at Port Elizabeth and at Pretoria against the Northern Transvaal. At Pretoria, Gibson played his best match and it was thought he had made it, but instead he slipped back and was just an ordinary player who never fulfilled his early potential. Whether he can re-establish himself in British conditions again, remains to be seen, but it is sad for he is such a pleasant fellow.

The injury to Barry John in the First Test at Pretoria was a severe blow and upset the whole balance of the side; there was no outstanding replacement in the British Isles that could be sent for, the best of them all, David Watkins, being with the Rugby League. John began the tour well and looked as if he would develop into the key attacker, for he had the ability to cut the line and straighten-up and make deep inroads into opposing defences. He could kick well and cover and would have proved more dangerous than Gibson. The South Africans hold this opinion and the back row men, Ellis, Bedford, Greyling and Lourens were more worried by John than anyone else. When John was paired with Edwards, then the midfield players had a chance, because the halves were positive and required attention from defenders.

One does not say that the Lions would have won the series with John and Edwards at half-back in all four tests, but they would have won the third test, and may have done better in the others. After the loss of John, came the equally disturbing loss of Edwards after two tests, for he may well have won the Third Test on his own, bravely though Roger Young performed.

There were other injuries which continually disturbed the side, and the loss of Edwards, Coulman, Young and Davies in four successive matches was a handicap no touring team could surmount. Throughout the tour, too many key players had to watch from the side lines.

Yet it was a happy tour, whatever certain sections of the South African Press and some sections of the British Press, reported to the contrary. The players were a happy group together and maintained excellent unity, for they never talked about or criticised each other. As a four-nation side they were as united as any future side will ever be. They enjoyed themselves and the majority of them were quiet, amenable tourists who were never any trouble to anyone, on or off the field. There was a small group of extroverts – this is necessary in any team – who whooped it up a little from time to time but were never guilty of 'unmitigated drunken revelry' as one hotel official stated. Another headline called them 'Lusty Lions: No Angels but not oafs', and while they did not pretend to be angels, they were never as bad as was suggested.

A long tour is a difficult thing to live through without breaking out occasionally and the decision to be taken is this: when and where? It is not always wise to whoop it up in public or in hotel foyers, but surely teams must be allowed to enjoy themselves? Lions sometimes broke glasses and paid for them; they occasionally broke down doors, and there was an amusing group of players who sometimes marched round the corridors at mid-night shouting, 'The Wreckers are coming', and most members of the party would then bolt their bedroom doors. The purpose of the 'wreckers' was to tip heavy sleepers out of their beds! The loyal order of Wreckers was launched at Mossel Bay and officially recognised at Salisbury.

Yet they were not 'hotel breakers', as was suggested during the tour, and all managers of hotels at which they stayed spoke in friendly terms about them. The 'burners' were a splinter group of the 'wreckers', their activities being confined to the ceremonial burning of shirts outside the hotel at Cape Town after the Boland match. It may have been a little silly, but it was the business of the Lions and did not interfere with the other guests.

I recall one touring team setting fire to a railway coach, and another turning on fire hoses to flood an hotel. There was nothing like that this time. As former British Lion, F. J. Reynolds, manager of the Cape Town Hotel where the Lions stayed, said, 'The Lions were no worse than some teams I have encountered in my playing career, and in fact not as naughty as some. Their practical joking was confined to their own team mates and travelling companions.' At the same time Manager Brooks had every right to say, 'We are not trying to paint a picture of virtue about ourselves, but we do feel our conduct has been wrongly represented.'

I wonder if the correspondent who wrote the article in the Johannesburg *Sunday Times* has ever whooped it up? If not he should do so sometime, for this would perhaps enable him to see the matter in a more discerning light. During the tour I attended many parties both with the players and without them, and their general conduct was as good, if not better than many teams with whom I have travelled. They deserved to be vindicated, and the more serious 'allegations' rebuffed.

If South Africa wants a colourful touring team to travel through their land and pour nearly one hundred thousand rand into the rugby coffers, they must allow for a 'little horse play'. To condemn a rugby touring team as national criminals is the surest way of ending tours. However, the Lions enjoyed themselves and their

relationships with South Africans generally was first-class. They
met many people; attended many schools, hospitals and functions, and visited many private homes. They met many charming
young ladies but were not 'womanisers'; and at least half a dozen
of the side never drank alcohol. Most of them preferred soft
drinks and milk, and as for running up large liquor bills this was
untrue except for the misunderstanding at East London, where the
bill was paid the next day. One presumes that a rugby touring
team, especially from the British Isles, is continually under
observation, and people not used to the ways of rugby tourists
are often 'disturbed' at the sight of giant, healthy young men,
enjoying themselves.

The management did well until after the Second Test, and then
the referees' 'troubles' blew back into their faces, and disturbed
them unduly. This was understandable, but they recovered their
composure before the end of the tour. David Brooks, a cheerful
character, was a players' man as he was always been through his
busy career as an administrator, and one cannot blame him for
this. Perhaps he should have been stricter and more 'aloof' at
times, but the players were particularly fond of him, and the Press
cannot complain, as he did everything possible to meet their
requirements. When there are 19 press, TV and radio corre-
spondents travelling with a touring team – the biggest group with
any British rugby side – the whole party is under observation
almost 24 hours a day. Some papers carried daily diaries of the
happenings of the 24 hours!

Brooks enjoys a glass of ale, as do most rugby men; he likes a
joke and a laugh, and is a bit of a leg-puller. He likes a party,
too, and anyone who knows the Harlequins, will appreciate the
point. David Brooks will always be 'one of the boys' in rugby,
and as a rugger man it is difficult to criticise him. All rugby men
have enjoyed themselves, and whatever faults Brooks may have
had, and they were not many, he produced an excellent spirit
within the side. I can only say that he afforded me every kindness
on the tour and was always approachable and helpful. I feel that
if the Lions had won the Third Test as they should have done,
David Brooks would be regarded as one of the more successful
managers. Of one thing I am certain, a touring team manager
should always be sent a second time in charge of a long tour,
because it is a most difficult task and can only be carried out one

hundred per cent efficiently, after the gaining of experience. The only way to gain experience is 'on the road'. I would make David Brooks the next manager to New Zealand or Australia. Tours are exacting, demanding, tiring, and never easy for managers. They are all deserving of our sympathy and not criticism.

Coach Dawson, who captained a Lions side on a long and arduous tour in 1959, did his best, as far as his capacity as a coach enabled him to do. He was a forward of considerable experience and produced a good pack mid-way through the tour, but did not enjoy similar good fortune with the back division. He was handicapped by the fact that from the start the backs were not of the same precise quality as those of 1955 and 1959. They were also badly hit by injuries, there was never enough flexibility, tactically, while poor Gibson never made the headlines in the manner of Morgan, Risman and Watkins. Anyone of these three players at their best would have improved the Lions showing behind.

Had there been greater initiative, things would have been better. The back play was too stereotyped, and many, many South Africans complained to me about this. Former internationals, by the dozen, kept asking me, 'What is wrong with the Lions backs?' It was generally too complex a question to answer accurately, as so many factors were involved, but I have tried to analyse it more deeply in the chapter on tactics.

One felt that throughout South Africa, rugby followers wanted the Lions to do well and recapture some of the glory achieved by the 1955 side. This team has become the yardstick for Lions sides in any part of the world, but especially in South Africa. Again South Africans have long memories, but they like to watch the Lions play, as much as their own players want to win. Several ground records were beaten on the tour by enthusiastic growds, and I am sure that had the Lions won the Third Test at Cape Town as they should have done, the crowd would have cheered louder than they did for the Springboks. Somehow one felt that the Cape Town folk at Newlands wanted the Lions to win.

Play on the tour was only occasionally dirty, with one incident in the First Test, one in the Second, two in the Third and none in the Fourth. The worst, of course, in the tests, was the blatant punch on Pullin that laid him cold at the front of a line-out in the Third Test. This was inexcusable and I hope the man concerned was admonished by his selectors.

There were occasional bouts of roughness in provincial matches, but the standard of rugby is much cleaner in South Africa than many other countries. It is only individuals who occasionally commit 'crimes' against the game, such as the player who tripped Gerald Davies at Bloemfontein; the forward who lashed out at O'Shea at Springs and set the chain reaction in motion, and the flank forward who dumped Roger Young at Ellis Park. In many ways it was an enjoyable tour on the field, and once one understood the reasons for the 'troubles' at Springs, one had the feeling, generally, that South Africans play hard but are not basically dirty. Many players agreed with this theory on tour and as Edwards often said, 'They go hard, and sometimes it hurts, but they are not basically dirty'. He can say this after finding himself frequently at the bottom of a maul!

South Africans play most of their rugby on hard grounds, and develop in the open air. It is a wonderful place for young people to grow up in and participate in all kinds of sport, and consequently they are basically harder than British players. I noticed this in the last test, although by that time the tourists were a little tired, leg weary and disturbed by the normal panic of the last week of any tour. I do not feel the South Africans are now quite as hard as the New Zealanders, because the way of life is a little softer in South Africa, a rich and rapidly developing country with a high standard of living for Europeans, and an improving one for coloureds and natives.

The mechanisation of industry and farming, and the amazing number of motor cars, finds fewer people walking and fewer players dedicated to training. At Stellenbosch there is the finest rugby training school in the world and the students there are dedicated, but once they leave this atmosphere, they become less dedicated. However, it is true that in some clubs in the Republic players are not selected unless they make an appearance at the twice-weekly training sessions. Few British sides would ever be at full strength if this procedure was adopted!

Thus although there is a perceptible change in the South African approach as compared with the 1920's and 30's, I feel that in South Africa, at least, the Springboks will always prove that much better than the Lions. This time the Springboks top twenty players were better than the Lions top twenty. There was not a great deal in it but enough to decide the series. Unless it is the decider, the last test is not a true indication of the relative merit of the two sides engaged. The first test was well won by the Springboks; the second test was drawn, while the third should have been won by the Lions had they taken their chances.

Had this occured then all would have depended on the fourth, and in view of the injuries suffered and the end of tour staleness, I still feel the Springboks would have won at Ellis Park and clinched the series. The result then would have been a fair indication of the relative strength of the sides, for the Lions were worth one test victory. Tests are generally won on errors, and referees' decisions, but in this series it could not be argued, despite the genuine complaint after the Second Test, that the referees influenced the result because of errors.

It is necessary to explain the referees' system in South Africa and why the Lions, at times, were concerned. The first thing is that a Lions team never has a neutral referee in any part of the southern hemisphere, and unless there is a complete change of heart on the part of New Zealand and South Africa, they never will. This, of course, is farcical, for the sooner neutral referees are appointed for all tests, the better will be the atmosphere of the game. I expect N.Z. and S.A. to oppose this violently, and already Tom Morrison and Danie Craven have said it will never happen. It *must* happen. for I have seen 24 tests overseas and I would say that neutral referees would have been a great improvement. At the same time I do not suggest for one moment that the home referees cheat or favour intentionally.

However, I am conscious of what Desmond O'Brien said during 1966 in New Zealand: 'Referees always seem to see what the red jerseys do wrong, but not always the other side.' It is difficult for a man to referee his own country in the tension of a test match. I would not like to referee Wales in action, and the Four Home Unions must impress upon the other countries of the International Board that neutral referees are essential for test matches. There are occasional referees who rise above this, such as Dr Bertie Strasheim of the Northern Transvaal, but they are few. Every side that goes to New Zealand complains about their referees, and this is one reason why a visiting side will never win a test series there. It is quite impossible to do so, but when you criticise New Zealand referees, the whole country is upset, for they cannot see the need for neutrality. If the southern hemisphere countries do not agree in future, then the four home unions would be quite entitled to have an Englishman referee England at Twickenham, a Scot at Murrayfield, and so on. It would certainly draw attention to the problem.

The Lions had genuine complaints at times, but generally on interpretation, and not on direct favouring. It would appear that every country has different interpretations of basic laws. This must be the experience of southern hemisphere countries when they visit the British Isles, and thus it must be the responsibility of the International Board to ensure a common interpretation. They make the laws and promulgate them to the member countries. The countries then decide upon their own interpretation of the law as written. Next the referees' societies look at the laws as written and add interpretation by their own boards, and by the time the law is put into force on the field it may be total different from what was originally intended by the Board. Again, the laws – by amendment and extension – have become complicated and tend to overwhelm and bemuse the referees as much as the players.

There are so many infringements now that earn a penalty against the offending side. There are so many infringements occurring at every scrum and line-out, that the result of a match may well depend upon what a referee sees, and can bear no relationship to the relative merits of the sides engaged. This is no direct reflection upon the referee, but upon the law-makers. At the moment, many matches are decided by the referee and not the players, and the sooner the laws are simplified the better. There can be no escape from this, for the law-makers owe it to the game, and the referees must be relieved of their dramatic responsibility, which is far too great. Occasionally referees like to think it is their 'match', but only occasionally. It is equally difficult for the referee to allow a match to run, and ensure the playing of every 'advantage', but I will say this that under the present code of laws, only the very best of referees can succeed in any country. Sad but true, and because of this I am very sorry for the modern referee, who gives his time to the game for nothing; rarely receives any praise, but a great deal of abuse. He is certainly one of the 'simple folk'!

A great improvement upon previous tours was the employment of the new substitution law, which helped the Lions on several occasions. This will benefit international rugby considerably in the years ahead and it will not be abused. It takes a little time to settle down and there were two instances on tour when it was not employed successfully, against Western Province and Border, but I am not suggesting that I would have done better than the medical officers concerned! Telfer and John Taylor were sent back on at Newlands after being injured when, probably, they were not fit to continue at one hundred per cent, and their returning to the field may have aggravated their injuries. Roger Young was sent back on at East London, although it was discovered later that he had two cracked ribs.

Obviously, a spot check is difficult, and often an X-ray examination is the only method of assessing the injury, but apart from these two instances it worked well. However, I would suggest for the international matches in the Home Countries championship that two medical officers check each injured player, one from each country. Indeed, I feel each country should have an orthopaedic consultant and a G.P. present at each international match. It would save a great deal of argument afterwards; NO player at international level wants to leave the field if he can avoid it! Another recommendation is that the four substitutes nominated should be changed into kit and wearing track-suits with ordinary shoes, so that they can take the field. The normal delay in South Africa on this tour was from eleven to fifteen minutes, which is a long time for a side to be one man short.

Arising out of the large number of injuries suffered by the 1968 Lions, one would suggest that for the next tour a qualified masseur or physiotherapist accompanies the side, and preferably someone from the four home unions who has knowledge of the British players. This change is long overdue, and as the MCC has recognised the value of such a person, the four home unions should not hestitate to provide an urgent facility.

Next comes the question of treatment of injuries, which is a vital point. Players move from doctor to doctor, hospital to hospital, and often different treatment is recommended. Everyone recommends for the best, but there is need for one central expert to deal with the players of one team, such as the doctor at the Groote Schuur Hospital, Cape Town, who as an orthopaedic surgeon won the confidence of the players and did an excellent job for them. However, difficult it would prove to be, in view of distances to travel, I feel that all serious injuries should be treated by one consultant. Central control is necessary and it would enable players to regain their confidence more quickly.

It is easier to achieve in the British Isles with such a splendid train and air service to and from London to the provincial centres. In New Zealand there would have to be one apiece in the North and South Islands, and in South Africa one each at Johannesburg and Cape Town. This suggestion is in no way a criticism of the ready help received by the Lions, and occasionally myself, from medical men everywhere in South Africa and other parts of the rugby world, but I have discussed this problem with consultants at home and abroad and they agree that it would speed recovery.

I recall one player on a tour having received fourteen different varieties of treatment and he became confused, lost confidence, and did not do himself justice on tour. Each doctor who treated him probably thought he was helping, but every three or four days there was a different form of treatment! High speed tours and constant air travel, and in South Africa, continuous changing of altitude, make things more difficult than they were.

I feel that there should be several more train journeys on tour, for they enable players to relax and take them away from the spotlight of publicity. Air travel has been speeded up and while this is a good things for business, commerce and professional men, it is not necessarily good for a rugby tour. Too much is attempted on modern tours, and matches in the week of tests should be avoided as soon as possible. There are too many centres now in South Africa with the creation of new unions, and naturally everyone wants to share in the hospitality and festivities. Compared with earlier tours, teams are now on the move constantly, whereas they had long periods at the main centres, and there is nothing like spending nine or ten days in the same hotel. Packing and unpacking and early morning starts, especially on Sundays, are not in the best interests of a long tour. One appreciates that some things are unavoidable but there is still need for great care on the part of the host and visiting countries in arranging tours, especially the travelling and accommodation side.

Firstly there should be no Sunday travelling, under any circumstances, and this should be one day of rest for a touring side. Again, all the folks met on Saturday could be seen again on

Sunday. Secondly the travel should be varied between air, rail and road, for variety helps make the tour more interesting and enables players to see the countryside and meet the people, outside of rugby football. Thirdly, only the biggest and best hotels should be employed wherever possible. Tours produce tremendous profits and nothing should be skimped.

Let me say, however, that all the hotels stayed at during the 1968 tour put themselves out to make the Lions 'feel at home', although catering for 50 increasingly sophisticated players, officials and pressmen, was often a difficult task for the smaller hotels, but they never spared themselves. Thus there can be no direct criticism of the hotels stayed at, or of the management and staff, but only of the S.A. Board and the local unions who selected lesser hotels in many towns. There were places where bigger and larger hotels could have been used, but there were NEVER any places where the Lions lived like TRAMPS. In some of the small towns there was a great deal of warmth at the local hotels.

The Lions occasionally incurred small damage to glassware, but they were no better and no worse, than many touring teams, and most of the hotel managers I spoke to, were full of praise for them. They did not disturb other guests, and never wasted food. There was no food throwing, or similar activities and in only one dining-room, at Kimberley, did they make any sort of mess. A point of note is that British Teams always enjoy being at hotels on the sea front, for this is a traditional way of spending holidays and travelling. One appreciates that this cannot be done at Johannesburg or Bloemfontein, but there are big hotels at these cities, although Keith Lamb and his staff at the New Skyline did a good job at Johannesburg. Yet the Lions were always enthralled by the Marine at Port Elizabeth and the Eden Roc at Durban, while Meikles at Salisbury still sets a high standard. Another that impressed me in many ways was the President at Bloemfontein where everyone and especially myself, would have liked to have stayed.

The Lions mixed well with the people of South Africa and did a fair amount of sightseeing. They were offered a great deal of hospitality in private homes, and players and pressmen were well cared for in Cape Town and in the northern suburbs of Johannesburg. South Africans are generous and they like to be liked by visitors. They are prepared at any time to discuss their problems

as a nation, but surely, by now, most other nations have as many
if not more than South Africa! They are conscious of the feeling
against them, but feel they are much more honest in their declara-
tions than many other countries. At least they cannot be accused
of a 'double standard'.

In each city the communities are small, and everyone soon
knows about everyone else. The rugby ground is a common meeting place. The white women have less work to do than their
opposite numbers in Europe, and many of them must find life
boring as their husbands are away all day, and their children at
school if not at boarding schools. The temptations are many; the
divorce rate is high in the cities, but especially in Johannesburg,
and alcoholism is also high. Yet it is a pleasant country to travel in,
and one is entertained everywhere generously, while nothing is too
much trouble for one's host. The people of South Africa still like
the British, despite the political climate.

I heard much from well informed sources that shocked me
about the British Government and its dealings in Africa, and
especially Southern Africa. I went to Rhodesia and found it the
quietest place in all Africa, the people more British than the
British. The people I met, ate and drank with, and discussed the
topics of the day with, were no more 'rebel' than myself or the
Lions. The awful truth of the unhappy situation left me sick at
heart. Indeed I felt more of a rebel than my hosts and if Air Vice
Marshal Harold Hawkins, chairman of the Rhodesian Rugby
Union, and Brigadier Bob Prentice, son of the late Douglas
Prentice, are 'rebels' then I must be a Soviet spy!

Fortunately, international politics did not interfere with the
tour, and the visit to Rhodesia was highly enjoyable and successful.
Throughout South Africa we were not worried by politics,
although guests at a special lunch at Parliament House in Cape
Town. I have always felt that South Africa, like all the leading
nations, needs a Ministry of Propaganda, run jointly by a South
African and a Briton. The Republic needs to present a better
image to the world and in the manner of the big nations, the more
propaganda you produce, the less likely you are to be criticised.
South Africa has attempted to state her cause too plainly. Now
it the time for her to say what she is doing for her native people.
It is much more than anywhere in Black Africa, and although
separate development may not please idealists, it may in the end

be what the native and coloured folk desire. The only way to decide on this vexed question, is to visit Southern Africa if opportunity permits and then say to yourself, 'What would you do, if you were domiciled there?' but not react like the "trendy leftists". One Commercial TV contributor visited S.A. for two weeks for the purpose of covering sport during the tour. He received full hospitality and every aid while there, only to produce, on his return, a strongly slanted TV programme with a political bias. As a well-known S.A. legal brain told me . . . 'You just cannot win! '

The travelling press party was quite the happiest I have toured with, and all members got along well together and with the team. The attack in the Jo'burg *Sunday Times* was launched by someone outside the travelling, official press party. I was surprised the *Sunday Times* used it, but it was not praised by any member of the Lions press party. They regretted it, even though many an Afrikaans paper liked printing the 'titbits' of the tour concerning off the field activities.

It was, for the most part, a happy tour. The failure to win the Third Test robbed it of its rightful place in history. Then it could have been better than 1962 and just behind 1955, and much better than 1966, while almost the equal of 1959. In the light of last season's rugby in the British Isles, I feel the 1968 side did a little better than one anticipated before they flew out of London.

CHAPTER TWO

The Cast

When one has lived with a group of sportsmen for three months and shared their worries and joys, it is not always easy to sit back and criticise them. The 1968 Lions were as cheerful a group of young men as I have met anywhere on my travels; they were always kind and courteous, and I gained the impression at all times that they wanted to do well and, most of all, wanted to win the tests.

They accepted the bad luck with the good. The injured players were full of optimism, while those who did not play in the big matches were the loudest supporters of the players on the field. They were deeply hurt by the unfair press criticism of their behaviour, the wound going deep. They did not pretend at any time that they were 'Angels', but they felt that as a rugby touring team, they were entitled to some latitude. Any group of healthy, happy, young sportsmen who can produce a profit of nearly half a million pounds for the host country, are allowed to 'indulge' occasionally in spirited behaviour.

Unfortunately those press men who criticised the Lions were not members of the official party, and appeared to write much on hearsay for sensational effect, but it did a great deal of damage. I feel that the various Unions must accommodate future touring teams, whether they be Wallabies, All-Blacks or Lions, at the top hotels, and the feature of a private lounge for the team must be adhered to. This would prevent a repetition of East London.

Nowadays travelling on tour is almost as difficult for management and players as it is for royalty, as there is no escape for a single minute in 24 hours of each day, from the all-piercing spotlight of publicity. The advent of TV on tour, admirably run by Dewi Griffiths and Cliff Morgan for the BBC, highlights every aspect of tour life.

It is no easy task for the modern tourist, especially off the field, and these 1968 Lions happily visited schools, colleges, clubs,

PLATE 1. *Above:* Big Bill McBride, the popular Lions lock forward, signing autographs on the team's arrival in Cape Town. Everywhere the 'plane touched down for the first time hundreds, sometimes thousands, of South Africans greeted the players. PLATE 2. *Below:* The first try of the tour against the Lions. Johan van der Merwe, the Western Province centre, has just touched down and left the ball as Rodger Arneil (6) is just too late to cut him off. Referee Max Baise indicates a try while Peter Stagg looks on

PLATE 3. *Above, left:* Did he score? This picture suggests that Maurice Richards, the Lions wing did not touch down properly in scoring a try against Western Province, but it was in fact a good try. PLATE 4. *Above, right:* The 'Judge takes a dive'. John O'Shea scoring the second of his two tries against Rhodesia at Salisbury, in a display that earned him a First Test place. PLATE 5. *Below:* The 'baby of the side' Keith Jarrett gets his first try of the tour against Rhodesia at Salisbury, despite a dive by full-back, Herman, to cut him off

and hospitals and many private homes. I found they were liked by the people and, unfortunately, the criticism emanating from East London, will mark the town down for 'care and attention' by future teams, which is a pity for it is a pleasant seaside resort.

These Lions were especially good with children, and signing autographs was never too much trouble for any one of them. They may not have won the test series, but they did not let the British down in any way, no matter what criticism you may have read by 'experts' who spent no more than two or three weeks in South Africa.

I know well what touring teams have to face, and how difficult it is to adjust to foreign conditions and atmosphere. There are moments when tempers are tested and sometimes even my colleagues in the press party went, in my opinion, just a shade too far, although well-meaning in their intentions. For instance, the Lions were never treated like 'tramps'; the referees' trouble was mainly one of interpretation, and the Lions side was suffering from weaknesses existing in the organisation, system and administration of the International Board.

Rugby Football's administration has not progressed speedily enough to keep abreast of our life and times, and each touring team appears to suffer somewhat from this 'conservative' outlook and approach of the Board. The Lions of 1968 did their best; they always tried and if their best was not quite good enough, then it should be argued that South Africa's top twenty players were just that shade the better than the Lions' top twenty. There was nothing more to it than that. Now to meet the cast!

David Kenneth Brooks. Manager. Aged 44. Formerly wing-forward and prop with Harlequins and Surrey. Company director.

Was selected by 'computer', as the South Africans say, for the job, one year before the tour, and devoted a considerable amount of his time with Dawson, his assistant, travelling the country, watching players, studying methods, and checking on previous tours. He was Chairman of the Selection Committee picking the Lions side and remained the 'boss' until the end when he said goodbye at Jan Smuts Airport. He knew then what a tough job it is to manage a Lions side abroad, for it takes a superman, with a super side to succeed – and Brooks came very near to succeeding. Had his side won the Third Test, which they should have done, history would have regarded David Brooks as an excellent manager. He was unlucky for he did a good job, and though more of a 'players' man' than previous managers, he held the party together. There was never any bad feeling within the side – they did not split up into four nationalities – while he defended them strongly against outside criticism. Obviously he could not play the matches, on the field, for the players, much as he wanted to do, and occasionally he whooped it up with the players, as did all of us who were on the tour. He figured in 'tough' negotiations with the South African Board over referees and interpretations and he confided to me, often, his difficulties, and thus I cannot criticise him, for my experience has taught me that managing a side overseas, especially a Lions side, is one 'hell of a task'! This Lions side were reasonably well-behaved and extremely loyal to the management. Brooks spoke well at public functions; at press conferences, and told many a good story in the 'bar'. Only a manager knows the power of the glare of the spotlight of publicity on tour. Before you attempt to criticise David Brooks, try it sometime. He had faults and made errors, but like all of us, he was human!

Alfred Ronald Dawson. Assistant manager. Aged 36. Formerly hooker for Wanderers and Ireland. Architect.

There was mild surprise abroad when Ronnie Dawson was elected assistant manager of the 1968 side, as he gained preference over many favoured candidates. However, everything turned on the interviews held by the Four Home Unions and their 'Prepared questions'. Whether or not Dawson was the best choice it is not possible to say, but no one worked harder at his task. From the moment he was selected, he threw himself into the job, studying every aspect of touring life and the approach on the field. He had been captain of the 1959 side, which almost won a series in New Zealand, and thus worked the 1968 men hard in order to get them fit. He suffered a set-back after the First Test but developed forward play of a good standard for the remaining tests. Perhaps this absorbed his time, for the backs did not make the same progress, but then injuries upset his best plans tactically, and poor Gibson never fulfilled the rôle of a 'midfield' general in the tests. A quiet-living tourist, Dawson worked hard behind the scenes for the team, and was most loyal in support of all his players. He was the first assistant manager to be given his head as coach of a Lions side, and had much greater opportunity than did

John Robins in 1966. Brooks, Dawson and Kiernan appeared to work quite well as selectors although, occasionally, certain players had to wait far too long for a match. Yet it can be argued that the pressure was so great at times, that the best available side had to be played. Dawson was an experienced tourist and had made 27 appearances for Ireland. His trip should now convince the Four Home Unions that a coach is a necessity on a long tour and that the next Lions side should have a month's pre-tour training, if it is to achieve more.

Thomas Joseph Kiernan. Captain. Cork Constitution and Ireland. Full-back. Aged 29. 5 ft. 10 in., 12 st. 9 lb. Chartered accountant.

To captain a Lions side is the ambition of all experienced players and although Ireland's Tom Kiernan had to wait until he was 29 for the honour, he deserved it, was the best man for the job, and did everything well on tour. It was not his fault that the Lions did not win or even share the test series, for he enjoyed a personal triumph, yet felt the sadness of all the party in not winning a single test. He had played 37 times for Ireland before going on tour and had been to South Africa with Ireland in 1961 and the Lions, in 1962, and thus was an experienced campaigner. He held the respect of his men, on and off the field, and had the magical charm of the 'little people' when he spoke officially, and a twinkle in his eye in private conversation. I never heard a word said against him, and his opponents respected him. He kicked 35 of the Lions 38 points scored in the test series, which was a new record for an individual player in South Africa. Kiernan was second highest scorer on the tour with 84 points in 13 matches, including one as a substitute scrum-half against the Border when Young was injured. In all his international matches Kiernan has scored 134 points and he told me at the end of the tour that he felt good enough for another couple of seasons with Ireland. He hated flying, and suffered in the Dakota trips, but he said, 'It's lovely to tour!'. He was deeply hurt by the exaggerated criticism of his team's behaviour, for his loyalty to his fellows was intense and sometimes moving, for it had the true passion of the Irish.

Robert Hiller. Harlequins and England. Full-back. Aged 25. 6 ft. 2 in., 13 st. 8 lb. Schoolmaster.

A popular tourist and a 'gifted' rugby player if not an out-

standing full-back, technically, Hiller was one of the successes of
the tour. He scored 104 points in eight appearances which is a
magnificent record and scored the largest number of points by a
Lion in one match in South Africa, with 23 against Border at
East London, falling only two short of the record of 25, held by
Malcolm Thomas of Wales after the 1959 tour in New Zealand.
His kicking, whether placing, punting, or dropping was technically
perfect, and an object lesson for youngsters. He was always cool
and played rugby in the Barbarian manner, thoroughly enjoying
himself. Occasionally out of position, he played his best match as
a full-back against Boland when under pressure. Known as 'Bossman', he possessed a dry sense of humour, and was a splendid
advert for English rugby.

Alexander James Watt Hinshelwood. London Scottish and
Scotland. Wing. Aged 26. 5 ft. 11½ in., 13st. 7 lb. Pharmacist.

Sandy Hinshelwood had already tasted the rigours of touring
when he visited Australia and New Zealand in 1966. Then he
scored 12 tries and was second in the honours list to Dewi Bebb.
He was a strong running wing who, like his three colleagues,
received too little of the ball. He was a good tourist, immaculately
dressed, who held strong Scottish views towards the game. His
hobby on tour was photography and several of his 'shots' are used
in this book with his blessing. Sandy played in eleven matches, including the Second Test when he and Savage defended stoutly.
I felt that had he been given more chances he would have
achieved much more. The tragedy of the tour was that in attack
Hinshelwood and his three colleagues, who were all above
average, were forgotten men. Extremely well-behaved off the field
he set an example to others and should continue to play with
success for Scotland.

William Keri Jones. Cardiff and Wales. Wing. Aged 23. 5 ft.
8 in., 11 st. 10 lb. Schoolmaster.

An unlucky Welshman who had little chance to show his true
quality as a result of a painful hamstring injury. He was the fastest
man in the side and a Commonwealth Games track runner but,
like Jarrett, was injured in Rhodesia and never became fit enough
again to win a test place although he appeared in two further
matches at reduced speed. This was a loss to the side and a
tragedy for a modest young man, who was a splendid tourist. A
schools international, he should add to his five senior caps, as he

can play equally well on either wing. He was paying his second visit to South Africa, and when really fit again, will concentrate on rugby football rather than on athletics. Is Welsh speaking, like several other of the Welsh members of the party. Had he been fit it is certain he would have enjoyed a successful trip, after giving up his teaching post to make it.

Maurice Charles Rees Richards. Cardiff and Wales. Wing. Aged 23. 5 ft. 11 in., 12 st. 9 lb.

Arrived in South Africa with the reputation of being a try-scoring wing, but he scored only six tries in 11 appearances and this was due to lack of possession although he should have got one in the last test. He suffered injury at various times, but was clever and elusive, often trying to beat three men with his jink and side-step. An excellent tourist who enjoyed his trip, he was amused in the Third Test that a Springbok should run across and kick him on the shin, twenty yards from the ball, saying 'Is rugby worth such an act?' He had played in Welsh trials for many seasons before getting a Welsh cap in 1968, as a member of Cardiff's speedy threequarter line. Richards was a shrewd and interested tourist and always keen to win. Now employed as an organisation and methods assistant with a keen analytical brain.

Keith Frederick Savage. Northampton and England. Wing. Aged 27. 6 ft. 1 in., 12 st. 6 lb. Schoolmaster.

After the 1966 tour, Keith Savage was misjudged, and even his club saw fit to discard him in 1967–68, which was indeed sad for both parties. However he tried hard for England in 1968 and was selected to tour again in South Africa. He set his teeth and decided to make a success of the tour. No one worked harder than Savage in his eleven appearances, including all four tests, on the right wing. He received small supply of the ball and got only two tries but one of these, against Boland, was a beauty, while he searched the field for opportunities and did noble work in defence. One hopes that he will be happy this season with a new club, for he was the ideal tourist. Immaculately turned out, he was the 'pin-up' boy among South African admirers.

Finbarr Patrick Kieran Bresnihan. University College, Dublin and Ireland. Aged 24. 6 ft., 12 st. 8 lb. Medical student.

Until the First Test, Barry Bresnihan showed form that suggested he would be the McRae of the team, for he ran and tackled hard and looked the part. However the First Test appeared to sap some of his Irish confidence, although in the end he made 15 appearances, including two as a sub, and appeared in three tests. A most likeable tourist, he just lacked that extra yard of pace which would have made him an exciting player, for no one worked harder in training and on the field. Known to the party as 'Doctor', as he was a final year medical student. Modest and cheerful he sang well at any party and was admired from the Northern Suburbs to Newlands. He toured New Zealand in 1966 and has already won eleven Irish caps.

Thomas Gerald Reames Davies. Cardiff and Wales. Centre. Aged 23. 5 ft. 8½ in., 11 st. 8 lb. Schoolmaster.

Was the most elusive midfield player in the side but suffered from injury and a lack of confidence in his own ability. Yet he managed to score two brilliant tries, one apiece against Eastern Transvaal and Boland, to reveal his true ability. Made an impression as a schools international in 1963 and has been up and down in form since then, but on his best days is a brilliant attacking player. One of three Cardiff threequarters in the side and most unfortunate to be tripped after grub-kicking ahead at Bloemfontein. This foul cost him a place in the final test side and was indicative of his unlucky career as a top-class player. A cheerful fellow on tour, he is now up at Cambridge for three years where he should win a blue. For the past two years he has been teaching in Cardiff after qualifying at Loughborough in P.E. Made nine appearances on tour including one test.

Keith Stanley Jarrett. Newport and Wales. Centre. Aged 20. 6 ft., 13 st. 2 lb. Employed by finance company.

Was unlucky from the very start of the tour as he could not leave with the party owing to an attack of tonsillitis. He played in the fourth match and was injured in the sixth and did not play again until the 14th, making only five appearances, which was disappointing for a young player of promise, although so well was he going in the end that he could have been tried in the last test. South Africans were disappointed that he was unfit, for they wanted to see the 'wonder boy' of Welsh rugby who scored 19 points in a match against England in 1967. Tall, well built and good looking, he enjoyed his tour, but wished he could have played more matches.

William Henry Raybould. London Welsh and Wales. Centre.

and fly-half. Aged 24. 5 ft. 9 in., 12 st. 7 lb. Schoolmaster.

A cheerful conscientious character, who readily accepted his fate as a 'reserve' utility player, while making six appearances at centre and one at outside half. A clever individualist, he found little scope in the close-marking approach of South African rugby, but took a great interest in the people and was one of the few players who attempted to learn Afrikaans. He was a Cambridge 'Blue', had experience with Cardiff, and seven Welsh caps while playing in the lively London Welsh side before going on tour. The first Lion from Cathays High School in Cardiff, and now teaching in Essex. An expert linguist whose brother is an amateur international soccer player.

John William Cleet Turner. Gala and Scotland. Centre and fly-half. Aged 24. 5 ft. 10½ in., 12 st. 11 lb. Insurance inspector.

'Jock' Turner had played eleven times for Scotland before the tour and had visited the Republic with the Scottish Border team in 1967, and was thus experienced and well-used to the conditions. He played in eleven matches on tour including one as a substitute against the Free State when Davies was injured. He appeared in all four tests. He was the most reliable of the centres in attack and defence, and the strongest, although he suffered from the team's tactical desire to kick in attack. Occasionally he executed the inside burst effectively scoring three tries, and dropping two goals while at outside half against the Eastern Province. Turner had a pleasant manner and happy nature and enjoyed himself on tour. His border brogue was attractive and he is another player who will serve Scotland well for several years. His club play him at outside half but Scotland at centre, and I feel this is his best position.

Cameron Michael Henderson Gibson. N.I.F.C. and Ireland. Outside-half. Aged 25. 5 ft. 10½ in., 12 st. 3 lb. Apprentice solicitor.

It would be unfair to state that Gibson was one of the disappointments of the tour, but by his own early standards he was as an attacker. He produced two excellent matches against the Transvaal and Eastern Transvaal sides, but disappointed in the tests, especially in the third, when his flair as an attacker was absent, and this accentuated the loss of Barry John. It was sad for the player and the side, for he was an intelligent, likeable fellow and a good tourist. South Africans expected much

from him, perhaps too much, for he was a slow starter, especially
after his early injury. In defence, and as a coverer and kicker, he
did well, but as the tour progressed, he completely lost the initiative to break or create openings. However, he can still re-establish
himself in the home internationals and perhaps take his revenge in
1969 against the Springboks. Was a Lion in 1966 and has played
22 times for Ireland as well as winning a Cambridge 'blue' and
leading the Varsity but it could be that his long career in the
game has blunted his fine attacking 'edge'. Made 14 appearances
including all four tests.

Barry John. Cardiff and Wales. Outside-half. Aged 23. 5 ft.
9½ in., 11 st. 10 lb. Schoolmaster.

The injury to Barry John after 15 minutes play in the First
Test proved to be a turning point of the tour, for no one filled
his place as a midfield attacker. He was injured at the end of a
long penetrating run and though it was thought that he would
play again before the end of the tour, he did not recover in time,
and finished with only four appearances. He was a confident,
balanced player, who looked from the start, much more at home
on the hard grounds. His kicking, running and handling was
accurate and he had time in which to do things, which is the
hall mark of a player of quality. John gave up his post as a teacher
to make the tour and returned home looking for a new post,
despite many offers received in the Republic. Although not a
schools cap he developed quickly as an outside half with Llanelli
and later with Cardiff. He now holds seven caps and should continue to form an effective partnership with Edwards, unless he is
tempted to join the professional ranks. A keen student of the
game, he talks easily about it, and was an excellent conversation-
alist at social gatherings.

Gareth Owen Edwards. Cardiff and Wales. Scrum-half. Aged
21. 5 ft. 8 in., 11 st. 10 lb. Student.

But for an unfortunate hamstring injury, towards the end of the
match against Boland, Edwards could well have been the top star
of the tour. This injury caused him to miss the last two tests,
after he had reached his best form, and revealed himself as a
scrum-half well-suited to the South African conditions. He scored
six tries in eight appearances and was a menace to back-row
forwards. His ability to break on either side of the scrum was
fascinating and when he played the Lions were a much more

effective force in attack. Again, his sudden darting drew the back-row defence away from midfield players and Ellis was never happy playing against Edwards. A brilliant schoolboy player and fine gymnast, he became the youngest man ever to lead Wales in 1968, and has a long career before him if he remains free from serious injury. He has seven Welsh caps and like Tanner, Willis and Rowlands before him, can earn many more. Edwards possesses an amusing sense of humour as when after the First Test, battered and bruised on the Sunday morning, he said, 'Eddie told me not to talk to the Press', as he imitated another tough but modest little Welsh sportsman, Howard Winstone. With Edwards playing, the Third Test could have been won, and is indicative of the damage done to the tour by injuries. He celebrated his 21st Birthday at Cape Town and was presented with an inscribed watch by his colleagues as a tribute to the man and the player.

Roger Michael Young. Queen's University, Belfast and Ireland. Scrum-half. Aged 24. 5 ft. 9½ in., 12 st. Dental student.

The happiest tourist of them all; a player liked by all and one of the bravest and most modest. Young never once complained and it was sad that he should fall victim of an accident, just outside the touch line, on the eve of the Fourth Test. This could have been avoided had the school children been kept back from the touch-line. It happened at Newlands, Cape Town, to Pask in 1962, and the S.A. Board should enforce a wider margin even at the expense of numbers watching. Young made nine appearances and scored two tries and figured in the match against Northern Transvaal. He was a strong player who suffered much punishment, and especially in the match at Springs, but always returned smiling. He toured with the Lions in 1966; has played 12 times for Ireland and was the inseparable friend of Edwards on tour, calling themselves the scrum-halves union. Their combination as 'twins' started in Rhodesia and I cannot think of two better tourists. Young, when qualified, may return to South Africa to practise for a few years, probably at Cape Town.

John Vivian Pullin. Bristol and England. Hooker. Aged 26. 5 ft. 11½ in., 13 st. 9 lb. Farmer.

Made eleven appearances as an efficient hooker, including three tests, but was rather unwise to play in the final one, for he was suffering from a heavy cold and could not do himself justice.

Pullin was an honest, hard working West Countryman, who struck fairly and did not deserve in anyway the criticism alleged to have been made by a referee. He enjoyed his tour, quietly, and like Larter went about the daily business of the tour conscientiously. Young was regarded as the quicker striker at first, and played in the First Test, but then came the minor 'witch-hunt' on hookers, and Pullin was given his chance which he took readily. Figured in the scene in Third Test when he was laid out cold at the front of a line-out by a sharp right cross. There was no apparent reason for this and there was no retaliation, for Pullin always takes the field to play rugby. One of six Lions in English pack, he farms in Gloucestershire.

Jeffery Young. Harrogate, Bridgend and Wales. Hooker. Aged 24. 5 ft. 10 in., 14 st. 1 lb. Schoolmaster.

One of the two hookers in the party who will remember 1968 as the year in which he married, won his first Welsh cap, and made a Lions tour. A Welshman teaching and playing in Harrogate, he learned his football in the Garw Valley and with Bridgend. Made nine appearances on tour and played in the First Test. He was accused, often, on tour of 'crouching' as was Pullin, and there was an 'anti-Lions hookers' campaign for a while in mid-tour. Young was strong, mobile and a quick striker who recovered rapidly from a wrenched back sustained at the end of the First Test. Was an excellent singer and with O'Shea did many a turn, while travelling by plane, and shared popular duet with the Welsh prop, 'He's the fella, Rockafella'.

Michael John Coulman. Moseley and England. Prop. Aged 24. 6 ft. 1 in., 15 st. 7 lb. Police constable.

This cheerful tourist developed rapidly on tour as a scrummager and as a runner with the ball in the loose. He became the peel-off expert and this manoeuvre became an essential part of the Lion's tactical approach. Coulman won his place in the Third Test team and then suffered injury after five minutes play, never to play again on tour, and the Lions had no chance of using the ploy. A loose-head prop, Coulman made ten appearances and scored a notable try against the North Transvaal from a peel-off which turned the tide in the Lions favour. As a policeman he was made most welcome by colleagues throughout South Africa and was presented with a Police blazer and many other trophies. He remained a happy, hardworking, modest tourist and should grace the English pack for many years to come. Anthony Laurence Horton. Blackheath and England. Prop. Aged 29. 5 ft. 11 in., 15 st. 2 lb. Area manager, wine trade.

A popular, likeable, well-behaved tourist who collected more 'nom-de-plumes' than anyone else and occasionally answered to 'The Major', 'Pinkie', 'The Gnome' and the 'Dwarf', but was an excellent fellow on and off the field. He played the first ten of his 12 matches at tight head and last two including the final test as loose head. He was strong and experienced and had played club rugby in the Cape when on a business trip there in the wine industry. Made three test appearances and was respected by his opponents. Was called 'Pinkie' since he could not get white shirts to fit him because of his large 20 inch collar, like the late Cliff Davies before him in 1950, and thus wore pale pink shirts as the next best thing. Paul Irwin christened him the 'Gnome', and Horton was the friend of everyone. During the tour his play improved immensely and he should continue to serve England, Surrey, Blackheath and the Barbarians, and add to his seven caps.

John Patrick O'Shea. Cardiff and Wales. Prop. Aged 27. 5 ft. 11 in., 15 st. 5 lb. Brewery representative.

Will probably be remembered, rather unfairly I feel, as the player who was sent off at Springs, but those who toured with him will recall 'Tessie' O'Shea as the comedian of the party and the 'Judge'. He was a member 'in law' of all splinter-groups, as the legal authority on all off-the-field activities. Each Sunday morning he held court and all misdemeanours were punished, with fines up to 50 cents, (six shillings), which were placed in the 'birthday fund' to purchase presents for Lions celebrating birthdays on tour. He was a good scrummaging prop who had his moments in the loose, playing extremely well against Rhodesia and the Northern Transvaal. Even when outweighted in the First Test against the jumbo-sized Springbok front row, he, with Millar and Jeff Young, conceded no tight heads. O'Shea enjoyed the tour; was a happy fellow, and bore no malice when sent off, not even pressing claims against the spectator assailant. His appearances were curtailed by injury and illness, and he made only eight.

Sydney Millar. Ballymena and Ireland. Prop. Aged 34. 6 ft., 15 st. 10 lb. Industrial sales superintendent.

The 'veteran' of the party, after touring in 1959 and 1962. Made nine appearances including two tests which brought his

tally for his career in three Lions tours to 44 appearances including nine tests, which is a splendid record for a prop, few
having played in the position for the Lions at 34 years of age.
An extremely popular tourist, he was much loved both by his
colleagues and his opponents. His 'activities' as a 'Wrecker' and
'Burner' were often exaggerated. He won a fireman's helmet in
1962 and a gas-jet cigarette-lighter in 1968, while he was the
court officer on Sunday mornings assisting John O'Shea. Whenever
he played Millar went hard and was a most solid scrummager.
Only once was he disturbed in front and then by a shorter prop
against Boland, although he lost no tight heads at the time, but
it caused Paul Irwin to suggest that the Lions should play a team
of dwarfs as a 'secret weapon'! Millar was always helpful to the
younger players and a close friend of McBride, O'Shea and
Kiernan. Says he will have one more season before retiring, and
may even add to his tally of 27 Irish caps.

Peter John Larter. Northampton and England. Lock forward.
Aged 23. 6 ft. 4½ in., 16 st. 6 lb. Technician in the R.A.F.

A quiet fellow, but an excellent tourist, who enjoyed his rugby.
He made 12 appearances including one test and never let the side
down. One of six English forwards on tour he should prove a
valuable member of his country's pack for many years. He was
unobtrusive, and not an extrovert, but did his job in the second
row and improved considerably during the tour. Had won six
caps for England before tour started and was a Barbarian. With
Bob Taylor is a member of the Northampton pack and found
the hard grounds of South Africa to his liking. He was a long
distance place-kicker, although called upon rarely, in view of success of Kiernan and Hiller.

William James McBride. Ballymena and Ireland. Lock forward.
Aged 27. 6 ft. 3 in., 16 st. 10 lb. Bank official.

One of the strong men in the side, but never one hundred per
cent fit after the First Test because of poisoned leg which troubled
him for remainder of tour. Was side's most experienced forward
with Millar; they were both on their third Lions' tour. Big, strong
and accomplished, he was respected by opponents. Made eleven
appearances, two of them at Number eight in absence of Telfer.
Was popular tourist and joint leader of 'Wreckers' Club with
Millar. Is alleged to have broken down a door at one hotel and
was then presented with a 'door' on his birthday at Pretoria! A

happy fellow and tourist with real spirit. Has now made nine test appearances for Lions and 31 for Ireland, while he may play on to beat Noel Murphy's record. A immensely strong player, he carried ably the mantle of Blair Mayne.

Peter Kidner Stagg. Sale and Scotland. Lock forward. Aged 27. 6 ft. 9 in., 17 st. 11 lb. Technical representative for I.C.I.

One of the biggest forwards ever to play in international rugby and certainly the biggest British Lion, with his 18 st. and 6 ft. 9 in. At first he took time to settle down and was played in the First Test as a 'gimmick' mini-lineout exponent. This was not a success and after missing the Second Test Stagg returned with greater fire, enthusiasm and expertise against Northern Transvaal and in the remaining two tests. Naturally, everyone wanted to meet Stagg and see him play, because he was to all young South Africans, a 'giant in seven league boots'. Yet he revealed patience off the field with the sight-seers and was a sound tourist. Already he has played 18 times for Scotland and played twice for Oxford in the inter-varsity match. An Anglo-Scot, he plays for Sale but his tour experience should help Scotland this winter.

William Delme Thomas. Llanelli and Wales. Lock forward. Aged 26. 6 ft. 3 in., 16 st. 2 lb. Electricity linesman.

The sole representative of Llanelli, the Welsh club champions, in the team and a modest, consistent, hard-worker in the engine house of the scrum, who made his two test appearances at tight head prop! An expert at the line-out, a worker in the mauls and a dasher in the loose, Thomas made 12 appearances including one as sub for Coulman in the Third Test. Was friend of McBride who invariably tipped him out of bed when the 'Wreckers' were on the march, but Thomas had a placid nature and was a most conscientious tourist. Spoke Welsh and attended many Cambrian Societies. While he has made two tours and deservedly so, Thomas has played in more tests than he has had Welsh caps, which number only three. Was in New Zealand in 1966 as an uncapped player and made one test appearance there as tight head prop and two on the 1968 tour, in the same position.

Rodger John Arneil. Edinburgh Academicals and Scotland. Wing-forward. Aged 24 6 ft. 2 in., 14 st. 7 lb. Textile representative.

If ever a 'reserve' or 'stand in' was fitted for star-billing it was Rodger Arneil, the good looking, likeable, amenable tourist, who was rushed on to the plane at London Airport before the team left as a last minute replacement for Bryan West. Never did a player accept his chance more readily or earn the right to be named as one of the six successes of the tour, for he was a tireless trier, and his play developed as the tour progressed. I feel he will continue his development at home and maintain a regular place in his national XV to become one of Scotland's outstanding forwards of the era. His manner and approach off the field were excellent and whether attending a party in the rich Northern Suburbs of Johannesburg, or escorting a young damsel in an-after-the-match dance, he was always the modest, polite young tourist. Arneil was a credit to Scottish rugby and his 12 appearances found him a willing horse in attack and defence. He and Barry Bresnihan sang many a merry duet and, on one special night, 'Little Farm' echoed to some delicate Irish airs!

Michael Gerrard Martin Doyle. Blackrock and Ireland. Wing-forward. Aged 26. 5 ft. 10 in., 13 st. 6 lb. Veterinary surgeon.

A good tearaway, let-me-get-at-'em, lively forward, who suffered because of lack of height and weight in South Africa. Had he been bigger and heavier he would have commanded a regular test place but gave way to Arneil and Bob Taylor. He made eleven appearances and was a most useful player, who enjoyed every minute of the tour off the field and was full of fun. He won a blue at Cambridge with Gibson, and had played 19 times for Ireland before the tour. Was in the Irish touring party in Australia in 1967 and should continue to serve Ireland for some years.

John Taylor. London Welsh and Wales. Wing-forward. Aged 22. 5 ft. 11½ in., 13 st. 4 lb. Schoolmaster.

Suffered, as did Doyle, from lack of height and weight but was further handicapped by a series of unfortunate injuries which prevented him getting into his stride, at any time during the tour. He was one of the really unlucky players, victim of an injury, a plague which appeared to hit the Welshmen more than those of the other countries. He played in the second match, and did quite well though injured, and then missed the next five matches. Then he was injured again at Upington and missed another five matches to finish with only five appearances. Despite his misfortune he remained a cheerful tourist and it is hoped that he will be fully recovered this season to help his club. A P.E. expert he was strong and fast, but never had a chance on tour for the reasons stated.

Robert Bainbridge Taylor. Northampton and England. Wing-forward. Aged 26. 6 ft. 2 in., 14 st. 5 lb. Schoolmaster.

One of the players most disappointed at not winning a test was Bob Taylor, who was a tourist, pleasant and modest, but devoted to rugby football. His mentor at home was Don White who wrote regularly to him. He suffered for days after missing the score, when blinded by the sun, in the Third Test and yet enjoyed touring. He was a quiet fellow, who enjoyed talking about football with anyone, and learned much on tour which should benefit his club and country. Taylor has gained much experience as a player with Hampshire, East Midlands, the Barbarians for whom he played against the All-Blacks, and with England in Canada. However his tally of only six caps means that his ability has not always been recognised. He can play at Number eight and did so in the First Test, but prefers the flank. In the old-fashioned set-up, he would have preferred the blind side. He made 14 appearances and also captained the side in the vital match at Springs.

James William Telfer. Melrose and Scotland. No. 8. Aged 28. 6 ft. 2 in., 14 st. 10 lb. Schoolmaster.

One of the strong men of the party who played bravely and well throughout, though suffering continually from injury. A true Scot and a sound number eight and pack leader, he played in eleven matches including three tests and scored three tries. South Africans respected Telfer and the pack was always better under his leadership, while his effort at Pretoria against the Northern Transvaal was as good as that of any player on tour. He has played 16 times for Scotland, toured with the Lions in 1966, led the Scottish Borders in South Africa, and should still lead Scotland for a few years. A keen student of the game, he called a spade a spade, and knew what was required. Big Jim, as he was called, believed that the whole purpose of a tour was to play rugger and go all out to win. That is why he said after the Northern Transvaal match, 'That was the greatest victory I have shared in!' Telfer's approach was admired by his opponents.

Kenneth George Goodall. City of Derry and Ireland. No. 8. Aged 21. 6 ft. 3½ in., 14 st. 2 lb. Student.

When Barry John was injured in the First Test at Pretoria, a blow from which the tour did not recover, the Management could not decide whether to send for another outside-half or a back-row forward. Eventually they sent for a back-row forward, as only one recognised number eight had been selected. The choice fell upon Goodall of Ireland who was not selected originally because he had examinations at university. He arrived in South Africa on June 18th, played his only game against Eastern Transvaal at Springs, broke three bones in his hand, early in the match and on the Monday was declared unfit for the rest of the tour. This was a tragedy for a likeable young man and a most promising tourist. A 'massive' was no substitute for a regular place in the team and, after treatment at Cape Town, he returned home before the official party. A great deal more will be heard of this young man in international rugby.

Bryan Richard West. Northampton and England. Wing-forward. Aged 20. 6 ft. 4 in., 15 st. Student.

After Goodall was injured, Manager Brooks cabled for a replacement and the four Home Unions put Bryan West on the plane immediately. Thus the 20-year-old player achieved his ambition and became a British Lion. He had been an original selection for the side, but withdrew with a leg injury the day before the party left, after breaking down in training at Eastbourne. He joined the party on July 7th, and played in two matches on the flank but was not available for the last but one match of the tour at Cradock, as he, too, was injured. Obviously, he will challenge for an England place again and, if he matures, may well make a future Lions tour.

Gordon Colin Connell. Trinity Academicals and Scotland. Scrum-half. Aged 23. 5 ft. 10½ in., 12 st. 6 lb. Insurance Employee.

The third replacement of the tour was Gordon Connell, a likeable, tough young player, who should play well for Scotland in the future. With Edwards already injured and Roger Young put out of action in the Border match, it left the Lions without a scrum-half for the last three matches. An immediate cable for help to the Four Home Unions was answered readily and Connell flew out to join the team without delay. He arrived in Bloemfontein on Friday evening, had a night's rest and volunteered to play the next day against the Free State. Despite the altitude, the travel, and the strange conditions, he did well enough, and in eight days played three matches including the last test with the spirit of a real rugger man. I admired his effort and compared it with that of Andy Mulligan in New Zealand in 1959. Scrum-halves are a special breed of men, and Connell deserved his Lions' blazer even though he did not receive it until he reached home!

Accompanying the party during three separate periods were the liaison officers of the South African Board in the persons of A. W. Retief from the Boland; Jack Horn from Upington, and Corra Bornman from the Transvaal, and all were kind, helpful and considerate. The baggage master was an old friend, Joe du Plessis, who was his loyal, efficient self and the Press party owed him much for their 'survival' on tour. The South African Travel Bureau had a representative in the unobtrusive Jan Venter and each provincial Union supplied a liaison officer to assist at their centres.

The British press sent seven representatives in Vivian Jenkins (*Sunday Times*), Pat Marshall (*Daily Express*), Terry O'Connor (*Daily Mail*), Ian Todd (*Sun* and *The People*), John Reason (*Daily Telegraph*), David Frost (*Guardian*) and myself. The B.B.C. sent Cliff Morgan as commentator and Dewi Griffiths as producer with a happy five-man camera and sound team.

The South African press was represented by Ace Parker (*Argus Group*), Paul Irwin (*Morning paper group*), Sam Merwis (*S.A.P.A.*), Gert Kotze (*Die Vaderland*), John du Toit (*Die Transvaler*), Gert le Roux (*Dagbreek*), Quintus van Rooyen (*Die Berger* and *Volksblad*) and Phil Saayman (*Die Beeld*). The S.A.B.C. had two commentators of experience in the field and covered each match in sound with Charles Fortune (English speaking) and Gerhard Viviers (Afrikaans speaking).

This was a large press, TV and radio party, but it was the happiest I have travelled with. Irwin was a raconteur and wit; Morgan a live wire, and Jenkins a senior 'deacon'. Gert Kotze was chairman of the South African writers and Pat Marshall, chairman of the British, and there was never a cross word between the groups. They, at least, had learned to live in harmony and had agreed to disagree!

CHAPTER THREE

A Tactical Review

A leading article in the *Cape Times* which, like the *Cape Argus*, *The Star* and the *Daily News* of Durban, is one of the leading English papers in South Africa, had this to say about the Lions after they had left for home: 'The Lions did not win the rubber. In fact they did not succeed in winning one of the four international matches. But their tour, which has just ended, was nevertheless, a tremendous success. A lively approach seems to have had a refreshing effect on our own play and all reviews of the series which have just ended seem to agree that there are strong signs of revival of Springbok rugby power... Luck was not always with the Lions. They suffered severely in the matter of injuries and key players, who might have made a difference to some of the results, were unable to play in many games... Their standards, honoured by time and tradition, were solidly maintained.'

The *Cape Argus* carried a leader which read, 'The undoubted success of the British Lions Tour can be ascribed to two causes. First, these great sportsmen went on the field in every match determined to play their best all the way and, second, South Africa's response to this type of play revealed a rebirth of rugby power that had not been seen for a decade of indifferent play and humiliating defeat... British rugby tourists have long provided a stimulus to South African rugby. The warm thanks of this country go with the Lions on their return home.'

These two comments are sincere and accurate, and sum up fairly, I feel, the impact of the tour on South African rugby. What good did it do for British rugby? One can talk of lessons learned, but we always talk of lessons learned and how, after trying so hard in adversity, the British failed, as they have done in so many sports in post-war years. We have become a nation of gallant losers, and there appears to be no way out of the valley of defeat.

After five successive tours with the Lions overseas, all of which

I have enjoyed as a traveller because of my love for the countries visited and their people and especially the close friends I have made, one must either be a sad realist or a cheerful optimist to continue to follow the Lions. So many times I have set off in high spirit, believing that success was in the offing, only to see hopes fade and defeat suffered for the same reasons.

Twice have I toured with Ronnie Dawson. In New Zealand, in 1959, his side deserved to share – and should have shared – the series, but for indifferent refereeing and the unfortunate injury to Risman; this time, in 1968, there were a different set of circumstances. I do not think we could have won the series, for South Africa were on the upgrade, as the leading articles so rightly state following a long period of defeat, but there was a chance of sharing the series, which only injury and failure to take chances prevented.

Manager David Brooks said at the end of the tour that the Lions would never be able to match the All-Blacks and Springboks unless they acquired the same tremendous 'urge to win'. He felt that it was this, as much as anything, which had helped to decide the current series, though he considered the 1968 Lions had been better prepared than most. He went on to say that what was needed in Britain was competitive play at all levels, and admitted that he had been 'hopeful, but not confident' of the Lions beating the Springboks in the series. He felt the Third Test should have been won and that the Lions 'had only themselves to blame'. When asked what went wrong, Manager Brooks said he felt they should have tightened up their forward play at the start of the tour.

He admitted that the injury to Barry John had proved a greater blow than was anticipated and he felt that this influenced the series. He would recommend that the Lions never fly home on a Sunday after a tour, but wait until Tuesday and admitted that the Lions had been treated with great kindness and overwhelmed by genuine hospitality.

Manager Brooks had been to South Africa with the Harlequins side, which is a closely knit club, playing to a traditional pattern. They are a force in the game, said to be typical of English 'rugger'; they have their moments and rise to the occasion when even the late Adrian Stoop would have praised them and allowed them some of the glory of the great pre-World War One days. Mr Brooks was selected by 'computer', as the South Africans put it, for the job of manager of the 1968 Lions side, quite the hardest job in rugby football. Make no mistake about it, there is no job harder, for even the Chairman of the Welsh 'Big Five' selection committee fades into insignificance compared with it. I have got to know the post-war managers, Ginger Osborne, Jack Siggins, Alf Wilson, Brian Vaughan, Des O'Brien and David Brooks well, and shared many of the troubles of a long tour with them. They all started in high spirit, and even if his tour did not disturb the senior naval officer, Ginger Osborne, only Jack Siggins, of all of them, was able to finish the tour in really good heart. True, he had the best post-war side under his command, but he also had the imperturbable Ulster spirit, that concedes to no man!

The others were faced with problems on and off the field, and are deserving of every sympathy. They had what it takes to make a successful tour, and were able to return home with a half share of the test series. Could the 1968 Lions have done this? Before the tour started, I believed that the side would do well to win a test, and if everything went really successfully, then the most that could be expected was a shared series.

As it turned out, a test (the third) could have been won, but I feel they would have needed to have played much better in the tests, and not suffered injuries to key players, to have won the series. Manager Brooks says that the Lions should have tightened their forward play early on. To some extent this is true, for they were greatly surprised at the strength and power of Springbok forward play in the First Test, but it goes much deeper than this.

Strange as it may appear, it was the backs more than the forwards that let the side down in the test series, after the First Test, when both sections were overplayed by a rampaging Springbok team. They were only kept at bay at Pretoria by the magnificent kicking of Kiernan. The backs were never really a test unit, and I feel that this must be said. I do not mean that they did not work hard on the field, but they never convinced the onlooker or the camp follower that they were going to pierce the Springboks defence, even when they got 'good ball' in an attacking position.

In 1955 and 1959, you felt that once the Lions got 'good ball' they would use it and worry the opposition. In 1968, this was never the case, and only one try came from the Lions in four tests and that by a forward. There are two reasons for this: (1) The Lions did not possess backs of the necessary high quality, although they were all good club players, and the best of them were often injured, and (2) British backs in recent years have got out of the habit of running with the ball at international level. Kicking has assumed priority over passing, and the 1968 Lions side could never run with the ball on the hard grounds, in the manner of players in the 1950's. In the mere matter of a decade, British back play had fallen away.

Once Gareth Edwards was injured, the Lions had no real attacking back – a player who could break the line – despite occasional bursts by Turner and from Davies on the rare occasions he played. There was no pattern in the back play which encouraged players to do this. We expected most from Gibson who, whether as a result of the overall tactical design or his own lack of confidence, rarely made an attempt in the tests to cut the line. Someone has to attempt it in a close match and the wings have to be fed regularly if no progress is made in midfield. What is so tragic that the Lions never attempted to run with the ball, with pace and accuracy, in the tests. This sad feature will remain with me always, as the symbol of failure of an otherwise happy and hard-working side.

Following the shock of the First Test, which even surprised the most hardened of Lions supporters, Coach Dawson worked conscientiously with his forwards and moulded them into a reasonable test pack, that did not concede at Port Elizabeth, and actually had the edge at Cape Town, although beaten again at Ellis Park. The pack developed good line-out tactics and reasonable scrummaging, but did not match the Springboks in the loose with the ball to hand. This gave an important advantage to South Africa which could never be neutralised, as all of their forwards could run easily with the ball and move it smoothly, while several of the Lions still appeared a shade uncomfortable with the ball in the hand. I saw Dawson work on this, and try arrow-head formation, but British forwards do not take easily to such manoeuvres which are mainly foreign to them on heavy British grounds.

I am not attempting to criticise individual forwards for their weaknesses in this direction, for it is a basic weakness of our play at home, and few forwards can expect to be as good as Greenwood, Morgan and Pask of previous Lions sides, as handlers in the loose and getters to the loose ball for continuation in the manner of Bedford, back again on his native hard grounds, looking so much a better player than he was for Oxford and Richmond.

Forwards need strength, stamina, speed, skill and HANDS in South Africa, and it is not easy to convert the average British international forward overnight into the equivalent of a Springbok in the loose. This is not an excuse but a reason, and it is the reasons for better play that are important. Members of the Home Unions, however devoted to the cause of the game and loyal in their service to their countries, still tend to gloss over the weaknesses of British sides in defeat, and prefer to praise those players and sections in the team who have done well. The reverse applies to New Zealand Union members and officials, and there must be a moral here somewhere. I like the members of the Four Home Unions, but were they to be a little 'harder' on teams and players it may help in the future. Individuals cannot be blamed for continuing Lions defeats. In the British Isles we are traditionalists; we always have been; and in many walks of life one adopts a conservative approach, without ever wanting politics to enter into rugby football. My experience has taught me one thing, however: that we must revise our whole thinking and approach, so that we get greater value for the effort that is being put into it by players, referees, coaches and officials.

We carry on in the same old way, much as the nation did at the start of the two World Wars, but in rugby football, we may not yet have reached our 'Alamein', when we will say as a nation, 'Enough! Stop there; no more defeats', and make sure our players are properly equipped and prepared mentally, not only to hold the enemy, but even beat them on their own grounds. Thus let us make 1968 our 'Alamein'. Let each of the four home unions ask themselves the question, 'If the Springboks and All-Blacks are worth playing; and tours to their countries are to be continued, then we must set about beating them, and ensure that our teams are trained and prepared with this end in mind, all the time'.

Our organisation at home is not tight enough; it contains too many well-meaning 'amateurs', who will not accept the happenings of sides abroad as inevitable unless there is a 'revolution' within their own administrative ranks. There are not enough 'professionals' in the sense that Danie Craven, Charles Saxton, Fred Allen, Vic Cavanagh, Izak Van Heerden and others are 'professionals' with a thorough grip of the modern game and all its complexities, and the hardness in approach that makes players 'live and die' for the game.

It may be argued that British rugby will never adopt this approach; and if this be true then we must not expect ANY Lions side to do better in New Zealand and South Africa than the 1966 and 1968 British sides. Yet we cannot change, immediately, the tactical and mental approach of our national sides. We have to start coaching and moulding the players in junior sides and working through the grades to the top.

To appreciate how difficult it is to get coaching 'through' to Unions and senior administrators one only has to read the story of the Welsh Rugby Union in 1968, for only a small majority of the executive voted, at first, in support of sending a coach to the Argentine with the national side, after that executive had appointed a full time coach organiser. It was still 'perks' for long service to manage teams abroad, until an angry annual general meeting of club representatives, fortunately alive to the situation, demanded a review of the situation. Then former Welsh captain, Clive Rowlands, a member of the coaching committee, was appointed, but then ignored from the national selection committee. Here is evidence enough of how slow will be the progress of the four home unions, in a change of heart towards coaching and the vital need of it, in order to achieve, eventually, better prepared Lions sides.

To have to preach the same gospel, after every Lions tour, is not a pleasant or enjoyable task. I welcome no criticism of individuals, but our system is outdated and in need of an overhaul. Fortunately there are a few members of each home union, who have 'seen the light', and who are prepared to move forward. Manager Brooks advocates 'competitive rugby' which has been the war-cry of colleague Vivian Jenkins since 1959, but much more than that is needed. Intensive coaching at school and club level must be the first major step, and unless there is a greater desire to run and handle the ball at all levels, a drastic alteration in the laws affecting the award of penalty kicks, as well as greater fitness, we will remain Number three among the big nations, if not number four – as I recall Australia beat England and Wales in 1966–67! We are noted in British rugby for discussing the problems and weaknesses, and then stowing away the problems, only to repeat them following the failure of the next overseas tour. When things are bad in South Africa or Australia, as they have been, then something is done about it. The Four Home Unions must act now!

The changes in the laws were intended to encourage attacking rugby, but these have been offset by too much restriction involving the penalty award for many minor infringements. Yet accuracy is the number one target for all sides in all grades. The 1968 Lions never achieved a high standard of accuracy in the basic skills, and here the Springboks held the advantage. For once, the place kicking of the Lions was of a high standard, and it was sad that the try-getting could not match it in big matches. Accuracy in handling, timing and running would have produced many more tries, while the neglect of the wings was tragic. There can be no excuses for this, and history will not accept any.

At full-back the Lions were well-served by Kiernan and Hiller, especially as kickers, and Hiller's achievement of a century of points was admirable in every way, while Kiernan's big match kicking earned him the new title of top points scorer in a South African series. Savage made a great impression with comparatively few chances, while Hinshelwood and Richards also tried hard but were far too frequently in the ranks of the 'unemployed'. Jones suffered hamstring trouble after the Rhodesian match which robbed the side of its fastest player.

In the centre, Davies suffered from injury and a lack of confidence, but could have been a greater asset had he been fit and in form throughout. Turner had his moments but, like Bresnihan and Gibson, was inclined to over-kick. Bresnihan played some excellent rugby in the early matches but never appeared to regain his confidence fully as a player after the First Test. Raybould had few chances, and did not find his best form as a smooth link man while Jarrett, following a good show in Rhodesia, was injured and did not come back until the closing stages, but could have been tried in the Final Test.

The tragedy of the outside-half position was the loss of John, for he appeared to have the necessary spark in attack as did Edwards, and whether or not they just happened to be Welshmen, they were more positive in attack than Gibson and Young, who throughout the tour did their best work in defence.

It was not a great back division, even when at full strength, but it could have achieved more than it did but for injuries, lack of initiative and the need of a more flexible coaching approach. If it had run with the ball and kept the wings moving, it would have done better.

In front, as always in a strange land, it takes time for forwards to settle down, and like a long horse race, the early leaders are not always the best stayers or the winners. The first six matches of the tour produced victories and those over the Western Province and Natal were well-deserved, but they did not reveal the weaknesses of the side, or how strong would be the Springboks, drawn from a pool of the top 25 South African players.

The First Test made a notable impression upon the side, and the pack was improved slowly, but never became happily acquainted with the referees' interpretations of the laws. This affected the Lions at the set scrum and the line-out, and while players in the end became resigned to their fate, they felt they were never allowed to develop. 'When in Rome do as the Romans' is an apt phrase for rugby tourists, but so many play by habit on the field, that they never adjust themselves before the end of the tour, to the difference in law interpretation.

Horton made a steady improvement as a prop, and Coulman took over from the 'veteran' Millar before his injury, while Pullin appeared the steadier hooker as Young was penalised for 'crouching'. O'Shea had his moments as a tight head prop but the Springboks test front row was a particularly heavy one. In the second-row the experienced and powerful McBride was never really fit after cutting his knee at Pretoria, while Stagg, following a difficult First Test, improved considerably in the second half of the tour. He fought much harder for the ball, while Thomas was consistent throughout though unfortunate in having to play in the tests out of position. Larter, was a quiet fellow, but a genuine worker who could become a much better player.

The Lions were not as strong in the back-row as the Springboks, although Arneil revealed himself as the tireless 'discovery' of the tour, as the last minute replacement for West. Telfer was the best pack leader and the 'driver' at Number eight, and Bob Taylor the most sophisticated flanker. Doyle, like John Taylor when fit, found that lack of pounds and inches were a definite handicap, however hard they tried. Goodall was desperately unlucky, and badly needed by the side, while West was too young and inexperienced to be of any real value at the end of a long tour, through no fault of his own. Finally Connell deserves a medal for playing at scrum-half in three matches in eight days, the first in less than 24 hours after arriving on the high veld, and including a test. He did his best and Scotland will see much more of him.

The best performances were the victory over the Northern Transvaal and the sharing of a draw in the Second Test. The best attacking rugby was produced in the first half of the Natal match, and the second half of the Eastern Transvaal match. The poorest display was against the Border at East London, but the only matches in which the Lions were 'over-run' were in the first halves of the two matches at Pretoria, and the second half at Ellis Park in the Fourth Test, but then only for periods.

Thus the 1968 Lions could have achieved more, but it was not a lucky side, in the matter of injuries and the 'rub of the green'. Luck is just as important to a touring side as the failure to take chances. Let us, finally, learn the tactical lessons of 1968, and say to ourselves, 'This is our Alamein, we must now go forward again into rugby glory.' We can, if we really try!

Coaching in all grades is needed with pattern rugby based on winning possession; using the ball; maintaining continuity of movement and improving support play. Only qualified coaches, properly organised and accepted can achieve this for the four home unions. Let us start now and end the long period of lip-service!

PART TWO

A Diary of the Tour
(May 12th to July 28th)

A Diary of the Tour

(May 12th to July 28th)

Sunday May 12

My third son Gareth and Les Spence saw me off at the station, and I was met by second son Wayne at Reading. We were late, which is rapidly becoming a habit of British Railways, before travelling by coach to London Airport at the cost of £1 a time, an indication of the extreme price of nationalisation. London Airport was busy, with as many immigrants in evidence as there were Britishers. The excitement of the afternoon was the arrival of Rodger Arneil in poor Bryan West's gear; the press conference was dominated by the BBC and ITV news interviewers who pestered Manager Brooks and Captain Kiernan with politically-loaded questions about apartheid and Rhodesia. It made one think that these two TV institutions were busy creating race discrimination rather than preventing it. Why do they seek continually to involve sport in politics? It was governments that withdrew their teams from the Olympic Games out of pure spite against South Africa. Who suffered the most? The coloured sportsmen in South Africa. One was more than ever glad that the Four Home Unions had accepted the invitation of South Africa to play rugby football and not create a wider gap in the relationships between the two countries. There were no protest marchers outside London Airport's terminal because few long-haired professional protesters know anything about rugby football. If the Four Home Unions play against Fiji in such close harmony, they must play against South Africa. It is as simple as that, for there is no place for politics in rugby football.

The S.A.A. 707 lifted majestically into the skies and after a record trip of 14 hours, including a 40 minute stop at the Cape Verde Islands, the giant man-made bird touched down at the Jan Smuts Airport, between Pretoria and Jo'burg, exactly on time at 0815 on May 13.

61

Monday May 13

The world's greatest living authority on rugby football, Danie Craven, and his able lieutenant Kobus Louw, headed an impressive list of rugby V.I.P's who greeted the Lions on a cold, misty, bleak morning. The Lions were made welcome with a short speech and then away by coach to the calm of the new and picturesque mining town of Stilfontein, 92 miles away, in the Western Transvaal. Vivian Jenkins and myself followed behind in a Morris 1100, a little tired because, smooth though the flight was, it is difficult to sleep on an aeroplane, even with the aid of duty-free brandy! The road out of the big city of Jo'burg rolls away across the high veld and the speed limit of 70 m.p.h. is easily maintained. The shafts of new gold mines reminded one of South Wales and Yorkshire, but the grey residue was in contrast to the black tips of Britain. The team had a quick lunch and a short sleep before engaging in a 40 minute jog trot on a rain-soaked pitch at Stilfontein. It had rained most of the day; a strange happening in this area in May, but British players were quite at home in the wet. Members of the press party crowded the players with questions and chat, and the powerful Springbok prop of the 1951–52 tour, Jaapie Bekker, paid a courtesy call at the team's hotel. The hotel manager, Nat Vogelman, was most helpful as were his staff, and one felt that it was right to start a long tour in a quiet place. Part of the evening was taken up watching an exciting film of the 1967 test series between South Africa and France. It revealed three things of importance. First, the bounce of the ball decides many matches in South Africa. Secondly, forward play is much looser without the normal heavy mauling, and thirdly mid-field players must do their own tackling. And so to bed for a deserved sleep.

Tuesday May 14

The Lions had their first serious practice on the local ground, one hundred yards from the hotel, and were watched by hundreds of enthusiasts, but weather remained dull. A phone call to my wife in Cardiff confirmed my safe arrival and an afternoon trip to Klerksdorp saw my old and faithful typewriter, known as the 'truth machine', safely repaired. David Brooks held his first full press conference to announce the Lions side to play the Western Transvaal in the first match of the tour, and he handled it smoothly, stating that he was always ready to help the press. The

South African party was suitably impressed and later it was good to have a heart to heart talk with Kobus Louw, who is following in the footsteps of his friend Danie Craven as a faithful worker in all parts of the world for South African rugby. He had been busy planning short tours for the future and during the evening he had a full discussion with David Brooks and the chairman of the S.A. Referees Society, Wouter du Toit. Details of the agreement reached upon the interpretation of the new laws was announced.

The first Lions side paired Gibson and Edwards at half-back and McBride and Thomas as locks, with Telfer as pack leader. It was a mixed side and an experiment, as would be the side against the Western Province for the second match. The four home unions agreed to the allowance of four substitutes per match on each side and that the names were not to be announced, but handed on a slip of paper by the respective managers to each other. Players would sit dressed in the stand and change only if required. The *Rand Daily Mail's* lively and experienced columnist, Paul Irwin, criticised his own and British administrators for this 'half-way' measure and asked what would happen if the ace place kicker in a side was injured with a few minutes to go, for his substitute would hardly be ready by the final whistle and a penalty chance could go abegging. There was news, too, that Jarrett was moving from Eastbourne to London and would arrive on Friday or Saturday. However the big event of the day was the magnificent reception given by the Stilfontein Health Department during the evening with a superb spread of food that saw the Lions really eat like their animal counterparts. This was prepared by Mrs Vogelman and her staff, and I have not enjoyed a better meal anywhere in the rugby world. A nightcap with David Brooks recalled many stories of the adventures of the Harlequins in Swansea. One he told against himself, for on arrival he was asked, 'Who's in charge of the party?' The reply came, 'David Brooks,' followed by a further question, 'Yes, but who's in charge of Brooks?'

Wednesday May 15

The dawn promised brighter weather and the Lions worked hard for 90 minutes under the direction of Ronnie Dawson who was strict and energetic and, I felt, purposeful. The forwards were really worked for an hour, non-stop, and then two sides played against each other for 20 minutes, the back play opening the eyes of South African critics. Edwards was lively and Gibson looked particularly sharp and I saw touches of the 1955 side budding in the crisp back play on the dry, springy, kykuyu grass. This was wishful-thinking, perhaps, but experience had taught me to be optimistic, and to hope that the golden tour was just round the corner. At least it appeared to settle one thing, that Ronnie Dawson would actually coach the side, although this was still a 'dreaded' word in Four Home Union parlance. Thus, win or lose, the Lions appeared to be more 'with it' than in the past, although no great sides are developed without great players.

Former Glamorgan player Jim Pressdee, now a successful businessman and cricketer at Springs, paid a surprise call in the afternoon, and it was good to see him again, slimmer and immaculately dressed. His salary was considerably more than that of a county cricketer, and his new Mercedes 230 would have been the envy of every Glamorgan player. He was supplying the mine compounds with cricket equipment and the orders appeared large and plentiful. Additional members of the 1951–52 Springboks met were Hansie Oelfse and Gert Dannhauser and they retained the admirable enthusiasm of that tour. The night was wet and stormy and the traditional weather of the high veld in winter seemed very far away, while there was news of many withdrawals from the second Springbok set of trials due to be played on the Saturday at Port Elizabeth.

Thursday May 16

The damp cold weather continued and the Lions visited a near-by gold mine to study the refining process. After this Manager Brooks and a few players went a-hunting and the Manager emulated Jack Siggins of 1955 by 'bagging' a Springbok. It was a good omen for the tour, we thought, and venison was served as an extra course during dinner. There were regular visits to the local florists owing to the charm of the attractive owner and one member of the press party was detailed to order flowers for the hotel staff as a reward for their kindness during the stay. The Three Fountains staff earned another 'star' for the hotel during the Lions stay and Stilfontein could become a regular starting-off point for future tours. At lunch Manager Brooks announced that Jarrett would join the team on the Saturday and so celebrate his

PLATE 6. Members of the British Press party with the Lions visited Parliament Buildings in Cape Town where they were entertained by the Minister of Sport, Mr Frank Waring. *In front:* John Reason (*Daily Telegraph*), Pat Marshall (*Daily Express*), Mr Waring, Vivian Jenkins (*Sunday Times*). *Behind:* The Author, Ian Todd (*The Sun*), Sam Merwis (*S.A.P.A.*), and David Frost (*The Guardian*)

PLATE 7. Mayor Josling, the happiest Mayor in Southern Africa, greets the Lions at Upington, shaking hands with the duty 'boy' for the day, Gareth Edwards. Behind are Manager David Brooks and Assistant Manager Ronnie Dawson

PLATE 8. The best 'party' of the tour. The singing 'braivelais' at the farm of Mr Owen Davies, Upington, where Jack Horn (left, with glasses) made his famous speech. Cliff Morgan, suitably attired, tries to call him to order so that Manager Brooks (centre) can thank his host

PLATE 9. The most tragic moment of the tour. Barry John, the brilliant Welsh outside-half, being assisted from the field at Pretoria after 15 minutes play in the First Test. His collar bone was broken

PLATE 10. Dawie de Villiers, the Springbok captain, passes out to his backs following a scrum in the First Test at Pretoria. Shielding him is Jan Ellis

20th birthday with the team, which was good news. The team left by coach for Potchefstroom and trained in heavy rain. Kiernan, however, remained on the side line nursing his injured knee and Arneil remained in bed with a stomach upset, while Pullin rested a sore back. Midway through the practice run Richards left the field with a bruised thigh but during the evening it was announced that Kiernan and Richards would play in the first match. In the *Rand Daily Mail* Paul Irwin had stated that the Lions were in 'Purdah' and not allowed to talk to anyone. This was a slight exaggeration due to a misunderstanding. Delme Thomas became the first Lion to receive a letter from home and he was mighty pleased with the local post office, while its cheerful staff worked extremely hard with cables, telegrams, letters and cards.

Friday May 17

The rain continued heavily through the night and early morning, and the Lions left for Potchefstroom not having seen the sun properly at Stilfontein, which was sad for it had basked in sunshine in 1962, causing Brian Vaughan to recommend officially, and myself in the book of the tour, to start off in 1968 at the new mining town. There are four mines there and they yield a combined profit of over £1 million a month from the sale of gold and uranium. However, Mr and Mrs Nathan Vogelman, the owners of the hotel, did an excellent job for the Lions and the press party and they were rewarded with many gifts. Vivian, Ace Parker and myself travelled by Morris 1100 to Potchefstroom and found the Kings Hotel had changed little since 1955. It was run by another member of the Vogelman family. The Lions 'rags' trained; Kiernan was passed fit and the evening was spent quietly although the British Sunday paper representatives were anxious about meeting edition times. I chatted with Ronnie Dawson and found him well-armed and prepared for his task, but, like us all, anxious at the outcome of the morrow!

Saturday May 18

This was the first match day of the tour and the morning was not without its excitement. The weather dawned just perfect for rugby with bright sunshine and a cloudless sky but not too warm an atmosphere. Keith Jarrett arrived at Jan Smuts Airport at 6.30 a.m., was met by Manager Brooks; driven to Potchefstroom and

C

sent straight to bed to sleep. While waiting for lunch I had a long chat with Jaap Bekker about the liquor laws and system of distribution as they apply to the native population. When the press gang arrived at the ground at 2.0 p.m. after a long walk, the Olen Stadium was packed and all programmes had been sold. Vivian's charming typist, Miss Scott, caused a flutter in the press box as she took her seat, and when the Lions took the field amidst cheers to start their tour, it was the SIXTH match of the day on the same pitch!

A win in the first match (See page 121) is always a happy event and at the after-match function the players were so much happier than they had been in Invercargill, New Zealand in 1966, after Southland had beaten them. Again history was made with the first employment of the new substitution law and Barry Bresnihan entered his name in the Guinness Book of records. It was Fiesta night at Potchefstroom and everyone appeared to enjoy themselves, eating and dancing, while midnight soon arrived. Gibson said he would have his injured ankle X-rayed at Dr Barnard's Groote-Schuur Hospital on arrival in Cape Town the next day, and Jock Turner would visit the dentist to have a tooth removed as a result of his receiving a punch in the match.

Sunday May 19

After completing our reports we set off by road for Johannesburg and had a hurried lunch with Ernie Franks before boarding a 727 for Cape Town. Sitting next to Tom Kiernan on the plane I found the brave captain extremely unhappy about flying, but it was a good trip down in glorious sunshine and the welcome at the Cape Town airport was a special one. Thousands of citizens crowded the barriers and reception hall to greet the Lions and the team members were delighted, for this was a real show of welcome. At the New Fairmead Hotel, Jeff and Majorie Reynolds were in charge and they were delighted to have the Lions with them, especially as Jeff had been no mean performer in the 1938 side at outside-half. There was 'secrecy' over the result of Gibson's X-ray and the Afrikaans press plus Paul Irwin were upset that the vital information was withheld, but Manager Brooks said he was awaiting 'further information' which suggested that it could have been serious. The boys crowded the 'Quarterdeck' cocktail bar and in the end when Monday morning arrived,

Manager Brooks, David Frost, Doctor Wells of Cape Town University, Charles Fortune, Vivian and myself were discussing philosophy. Vivian's thoughts on life were a little more than amusing!

Monday May 20

It was a beautiful autumnal day in Cape Town, and there can be few better anywhere in the world. The team paid their first visit of the tour to Newlands for training and were welcomed by the heart-transplant patient, Dr Phillip Blaiberg. He chatted gaily with the boys, posed for photographs and even executed a few passes to reveal the remarkable miracle of surgery. He looked well and even spoke a few phrases in Welsh but was not allowed to shake hands with anyone; neither was he allowed to attend the match. I spoke to members of the R.A.F. Association at lunch time, with my good friend Vivian Duggan in the chair, and then did some shopping in the City. The backcloth of the remarkable Table Mountain was covered with its tablecloth of cloud and it was easy to realise why the whole scene impressed Sir Francis Drake when he first saw it and uttered the words: 'The fairest cape in all the world.' His words still ring true and being sent to Cape Town to live and work would be no punishment for any journalist. During the evening the British team and journalists were the guests of the British Ambassador and his wife, Sir John and Lady Nicholls. One of the happiest receptions of its kind, it was good to make contact with the Naval attaché, Commander (E) Stephen Sharratt, and he invited David Brooks and myself to pay a courtesy call on one of Her Majesty's ships, during our second visit to the city.

Tuesday May 21

Highlight of the day was lunch at Parliament Building as the guest of the Minister of Sport, Mr Frank Waring, who was an outstanding Springbok in 1931. A seven course meal, perfectly cooked and delightful served, pleased the Lions and the British Press in the tall, spacious dining-room, around which hung giant oil paintings of the leading South African prime ministers, starting with Cecil Rhodes. Unfortunately Mr John Vorster was ill and unable to attend the lunch but we heard good reports of him on all sides and that his more 'liberal' approach would, in the end, pay dividends for South Africa. After lunch we sat in the visitors gallery for half an hour and listened to question time. Both languages were spoken but the Speaker, with his sharp comments, kept a firm control on the proceedings. Personally, I listened closely to Mrs Helen Susman, the one independent M.P., for I had met her at the Mayor's luncheon at Kitwe in 1955, when she was *en route* to the Congo to study conditions there. During the evening I had dinner with Vivian Duggan and his family and heard much about the delights of the Cape and how sad the British stock in the area were at the attitude of the British Government. As he said, 'I am sure South Africa would buy more and more from Britain and help the export drive, if there was better relationship and understanding.' He is right, for Britain needs to be more realistic to survive.

Wednesday May 22

It was Newlands' day and the second match of the tour, a hard one against the Western Province. A visit to the *Cape Argus* office found Ace Parker busy at work and there are few more prolific writers on the game. He is a shrewd observer and a fair critic with a big following in South Africa. It was a perfect autumn day, warm and sunny, almost too hot for rugby, but the match was exciting if not outstanding in quality, and the Lions achieved a notable victory that boosted their morale. It was so different from suffering defeat at Invercargill and Dunedin in 1966. There were more injuries and discussions about the substitution law, but Jeff Reynolds and his staff laid on an excellent after-the-match meal at the New Fairmead, and the evening was thoroughly enjoyed by all.

Thursday May 23

The Lions made an early start and set off in two planes for Oudtshoorn where a visit was made to the Cango Caves and an ostrich farm. Another excellent lunch was provided at the Caves and Keith Jarrett proved the best ostrich rider while John O'Shea ran an impromptu 'Carol Levis discovery' concert on the coach, won by Barry Bresnihan with a typical Irish number. The coach ride from Oudtshoorn to Mossell Bay was in the reverse direction to the memorable ride of 1955, described in *Lions on Trek*. The road over the Robinson Pass is now much improved and there were no alarms, before we settled in peacefully at the Santos Hotel at Mossell Bay, looking out over the historic Bay and the Indian Ocean. The Lions, at least the more energetic ones, went for an evening swim, but most retired early to bed for there had not been a great deal of sleep enjoyed in Cape Town. The tour was settling down into routine and at this stage the Lions were happy even though five players, Gibson, Turner, Davies, Telfer and John Taylor, had been left behind at Cape Town for treatment. A wise precaution.

Friday May 24

A quiet day at Mossell Bay with plenty of work done and a walk round the town with a special visit to the historical post office tree where ancient Portugese navigators used to leave messages. It is now a posting box in the form of a shoe, as the original messages were left in a navigator's boot, and is a national monument. The first contact with the area by Europeans was in 1488 and now Mossell Bay is one of the principle holiday resorts in the Cape. The average rainfall is less than $1\frac{1}{2}$ inches per month and there is very safe bathing there, while the variation in temperature between summer and winter is 12 degrees. The main railway line ran in front of the hotel and it gave me much delight to see steam trains in action again. The lure of steam is all embracing! David Brooks, Vivian and myself enjoyed dinner at the home of former Oxford University captain, Nelles Vintcent and his charming wife Pip, together with two friends. This was indeed pleasant and amusing.

Saturday May 25

This was the warmest day of the tour to date and there were many swimmers in the early morning. Photographers were out in strength and cars were arriving at the ground at 8.0 a.m. for a 4.0 p.m. kick-off, which is an indication of the enthusiasm in the area for rugby football and the pleasure anticipated in watching the Lions. The total population of Mossell Bay is 15,000 including Europeans, Coloureds and Bantus. At the ground for the match against South Western districts were 7,500 Europeans and 2,500 Coloureds, the latter being most enthusiastic supporters of the Lions. Another victory was gained and only one injury suffered, by Delme Thomas, with a badly bruised toe. The report to the

BBC was loud and clear and it was good to tell the rain-drenched folk at home that the sun was blazing down at Mossell Bay. The after-match reception was pleasant and one detected the light of success in the eyes of the Lions for their start, at this stage, was the best by a post-war British team in South Africa. Former Springbok hooker, Abe Malan confided to me, 'They are a very fast side, and if they keep the ball moving they will worry the Springboks.' The players did not retire early and there was a great deal of door-banging and turning over of beds. Obviously the tour was coming alive and the spirit was good, but the threat of injuries was still very real. No side in South Africa escapes injuries, no matter how clean the play, and these must be associated with the hard grounds.

Sunday May 26

We said good bye to the pleasant town of Mossell Bay and set off early from the neighbouring town of George in two DC 3s. Several players were upset by the bumpy ride caused by a strong headwind, and there was a stop in a field at beautiful Plattenburg Bay for mail before reaching Port Elizabeth at midday. The 'Garden Route', as it is called, looked tempting as we flew along the beaches and we were told that a large number of former British army officers live there in splendid retirement. Who can blame them – in peace and quiet away from the battlefield, although not too far to the north-west is Ladysmith, the scene of the siege in the Boer War.

There was a pleasant welcome awaiting the Lions in the friendly city of Port Elizabeth, and many old friends including Boete Erazmus, Lawton Fourie, Neil Cameron, Jimmy Ward and Fronnie Froneman. There was no wind blowing and the sun shone strongly while the sea looked just as inviting as ever from the wide windows of the Marine Hotel. Of all headquarters on Lions tours this is probably the most pleasant, although the Arthur's Seat Hotel at Seapoint in Cape Town, as a four star hotel, has few rivals.

Port Elizabeth was celebrating the first home-made South African motor car when we arrived and the city was noticeably busier following an interval of four years. It is one of the five major cities in the republic and the centre of the wool and fruit exporting. The 1820's settlers there are to be commemorated with a special monument at Grahamstown, and as English speaking pioneers they will then be recognised, as have already the Voortrekkers, Huguenots and early German settlers. It was fitting that the Prime Minister should make an appeal on the national network of the S.A.B.C. for £750,000 to create the monument, if possible, by 1970, exactly 150 years after the gallant four thousand pioneers arrived from England.

Monday May 27
Another day of glorious sunshine that set Port Elizabeth alight and caused the wave tops to flash and glisten as they pounded inshore towards the Marine Hotel. The Lions trained in a temperature well above 70 degrees, and Gibson, running for the first time, ran straight into one of the uprights as the party jog-trotted round the Boete Erazmus. A lump developed on his forehead, the size of an egg, but after receiving attention he was out again, training and enjoying the warm sun. During the evening the Lions were the guests of the Lord Mayor at the City Hall and many old friends were present including Helen and Jimmy White, George Smith and Popeye Strydom who are former Springboks, and a few Welsh folk who had recently emigrated from the Principality.

Tuesday May 28
Weather continued perfectly and it was pleasant to take lunch at the Port Elizabeth Club with Peter Huggett who called himself a 'rebel from Rhodesia'. In the lunch party was Mac Pollock, the proud father of the two test cricketing sons, Peter and Graeme. There were still no letters from home for me, and this brought back the loneliness of the war, when everyone waited for letters and the good news that Nazi bombs had not reached one's families. I despatched a cable to 'the Towers' as a check. In the evening Cliff Morgan and Dewi Griffiths enlivened the lounge at the Marine Hotel with a traditional Welsh rugby sing-song and the Managers, Brooks and Dawson, joined in. Paul Irwin was a great success as the third 'bar' of a special Russian number devised by Griffiths.

Wednesday May 29
Another match day that dawned beautifully, and most of the press party went for a swim. Fortunately we were able to arrange

the use of the Telex system for the Thomson Group morning papers, but after the match *v*. Eastern Province, in which the Lions appeared to falter at one stage, the poor post office telegraphists were 'smoked-out' as local officials prepared for the evening braievlais. A cable came back from the 'Towers' that all was well, and so at dinner a special bottle of South African wine was opened. The quality of the wine in the Republic is excellent and in consultation with Charles Fortune and other connoisseurs, we drafted a list of the better South African wines for future reference. They are cheaper in the UK than French wines and I recommend them.

Thursday May 30

Everyone had been most friendly in Port Elizabeth and Jimmy Ward and Lawton Fourie did everything possible to ensure that we were happy. This is most important for the players and the travelling press. We set off by plane for Durban and there many friends greeted us, including two of long standing, Reg Sweet and Izak van Heerden, whose war records make one feel pleased to have them as friends. It was good to be back at the Eden Roc Hotel where so many touring teams have enjoyed pleasant stays and to see so many of the staff still in action under happy management. During the evening I had an excellent meal at the lovely home of John and Joan Lewis, up on the heights at back of the city. Staying with them were Hector and Enid Thomas, good friends from Cardiff on their first holiday to South Africa and, as they said, not their last! Like other friends of mine they were on holiday to see South Africa for themselves and like many, were agreeably surprised. As a well-known Welsh medical consultant, Hector was interested in the medical services. The news of the day was confined to whether the Lions would make the trip to Rhodesia as the UN had agreed to complete sanctions against the country, but Manager Brooks said he was determined to go to fulfil a long-standing promise to Rhodesian rugby men, because the Lions did not wish to interfere with politics. The Government at home did not wish them to go, but at this stage, could not stop them. It was not the intention of the Lions, as law-abiding citizens, to disobey the wishes of the government, but they wanted to play rugby against people they liked. South African papers gave the issue a good show and the British press cabled back meaty cables

PLATE 11. *Above:* The Lions v. Transvaal. Gerald Davies takes the ball after Kiernan has tackled Nomis, Transvaal's Springbok centre, with a half-nelson.
PLATE 12. *Below:* Delme Thomas, the Lions lock, indicates how hard it is on the high veld when he stops the charging Transvaal wing, Nortje

PLATE 13. *Above:* Relaxing before the Second Test. Fearless Barry Bresnihan shows he has no fear of snakes at the Port Elizabeth Snake Pit. Watching him carefully are Peter Stagg (*left*) and Tom Kiernan. Bresnihan showed the same lack of fear in his tackling in the Second Test. PLATE 14. *Below:* Tommy Bedford, the Springbok number eight and pack leader, just escapes the clutches of Bresnihan and Savage as he dashes away in the Second Test at Port Elizabeth

but all were of the opinion that the Lions should go, and only a direct 'order in council' from the British government should stop them doing so.

Friday May 31

Another pleasant day that was not too warm or humid, although good enough for a summer's day at home. Reg Sweet and his wife had lunch with Cliff Morgan and myself and discussed the highlights of 1955, before the Lions party went to the Races. This was great fun. Unfortunately as I was about to put a few rand on a horse, Blue Tavernier, the window of the tote came down and the bell rang for the start of the main race. Cliff had travelled to Durban with the owner and it was a hot tip. Naturally, the horse won, and paid 16 rand for one rand, and Morgan and Thomas had missed the bus! We did a little better on the next race but it was Jenkins who 'cleaned up' on the last. Hector Thomas did quite well and the Stewards were extremely kind to all visitors. During the evening David Brooks spoke exceedingly well at the Duikers Rugby Club dinner and it was good to meet many friends of former tours including four judges, two of whom spoke with amusing freedom. The Duikers are the Barbarians of Natal and do a great deal of good to foster the right spirit in the game.

Saturday June 1

Yet another match day dawned well but by the end of the afternoon it was blowing a gale to indicate how quickly the weather can change on the coast in Southern Africa. The Lions were worried after breakfast that it would be too hot but it was considerably cooler after lunch and the players took the field for the match *v.* Natal in good heart. Vivian and myself had a pleasant lunch with Valerie Compton, her sister Joan and other friends before moving on to the ground, and the first half provided the best rugby of the tour up to that time. Edwards and John were in fine form and Natal looked like being overwhelmed but they survived and battled back to a storming rally which pinned down the Lions in defence. It was noisy and exciting, and in keeping with the brave rallying power of Natal. The after-match party was held in a marquee on an adjoining ground and the 'big top' did well to survive the gale of wind.

Sunday June 2

There was excitement in the air, and one could sense it, as we said farewell to hospitable Durban hosts and flew north to Rhodesia. It was a voyage of adventure to a 'rebel' land, or so we had been led to believe. We wanted to see for ourselves, and judge the situation. Was this lovely country, where we had travelled on several occasions, as rebellious as many would have had us believe? The president of its Rugby Union, Air Vice-Marshall Harold Hawkins, Commandant of the Rhodesian Air Force, had spent some time on Saturday evening outlining the situation but, as he said, 'See for yourselves!' When we arrived at Salisbury it was just getting dark but we could see the flags spread out over the balcony of the airport (one of them was the Welsh flag!), as hundreds of people, so many of them of British birth, shouted 'Thanks for coming!' It was quite emotional. How could we rugby players and followers from Britain, be at logger-heads with these people, who are more British than the British? As we drove to Meikles Hotel, with its new and specious wing to make it one of the big hotels of the old Commonwealth, we found everything so calm. We saw few if any police; there were no restrictions, and we had a fine welcome from local officials at a reception. The speeches made were non-controversial and a meal with Len Pincher and his wife was both enjoyable and informative. It provided the best steak fillet in Southern Africa and much information about Malawi and Zambia as well as Rhodesia. Zambia is moving rapidly 'Red' under Russian and Chinese influence, while Banda in Malawi is attempting to come to terms with Southern Africa. Some half a million of his people are employed in South Africa and are a source of foreign revenue for his country. Then late at night, we heard from friends, of many years standing, of the atrocities in the Congo and Nigeria. They were both fantastic and ghastly and proof enough that all development in Africa must be gradual.

Monday June 3

At the reception on the previous day Cliff Morgan and myself had been invited to do the first full TV rugby commentary staged in Rhodesia and the young producer, Martin Lock, who had spent a few years with commercial TV in the UK was most pleased that we accepted. The day dawned well again, and the luck of the Lions in this respect on match days, continued gaily. The TV platform and Press box were up high, on temporary stilts, at the back of the main stand, rather cramped but providing an excellent view. Mr Ian Smith arrived during one of the 'curtain-raisers' and took his seat with Mrs Smith, without pomp and ceremony. Then the Lions entered the Police Ground, to walk to their dressing-room and every one in the crowd stood and cheered and clapped. It was quite spontaneous and from the heart. How could these fine people be classed as rebels? The Lions struggled for an hour and then cut loose to provide some dazzling running rugby that was warmly appreciated. Unfortunately it grew bitterly cold and typing out our cables in the dark with the aid of a miner's lamp was a new experience! At the reception after the match Ian Smith moved freely and unobtrusively to chat with members of the Lions party, who liked him. There was a light in his eyes; the light of a man living for his country. At dinner at Meikles and later at the Salisbury Sports Club there was an atmosphere of togetherness, and if the Lions were giving 'comfort and aid' to a rebel state then I wanted, very much, to be part of it. The singing was excellent and, later, in the early hours at the home of George Pitt who was a long-range desert man in World War II, the host and Freddie Dawes, a former Wasps player and tobacco farmer, told Vivian, Cliff and myself of the real Rhodesia. It was a case of meeting the people, and one could understand why Mr Harold Wilson was not popular in Rhodesia. The withdrawal of the MCC visit was a bitter blow, yet we gained the impression that a settlement could be achieved if politicians would for-feit just a little personal pride in the cause of world under-standing.

Tuesday June 4

Before leaving Salisbury, Cliff and myself gave a long TV interview about rugby tours and our ideas on the game, and then a quick lunch at the spacious Salisbury Club before returning to Pretoria by plane. It was sad to leave the 'rebel' country where we had re-discovered such warmth and friendliness, but the Lions party had seen for themselves and were satisfied that it was not too late to settle the problem. The sadness of the whole situation was that Britain had passed the problem to the UN. It could, and should, have been settled privately and enforcing 'sanctions'

appeared a petty method of bringing what could have remained
as a 'very loyal', Rhodesia to its knees. The plane was delayed at
the airport owing to a late arrival and it was dark and extremely
cold when we reached Pretoria. The hotel was certainly friendly
but my feeling was that the South African Board perhaps could
have done better for the Lions, who were attracting a 75,000 gate
at Loftus Versveld for the test, with receipts well over £100,000.
However a good night's sleep was had by all and it was good to
find my room warmer than most, but there were still no letters
from home. At least eight must have been floating round the
Republic in search of me!

Wednesday June 5

The Lions practised in perfect conditions at Loftus Versveld
after the test fifteen had been selected. There were surprise choices
in O'Shea, Stagg and Telfer at forward while Savage received
preference over Hinshelwood, to become the only Englishman in
the side, and he without a club! Telfer had not played since the
Cape Town match and Horton had played hard and well, only to
lose the tight head post 'at the bell'. At the afternoon press
conference Manager Brooks expressed every confidence that Telfer
was fit and that only five players, John Taylor, John Pullin, Keith
Jarrett, Keri Jones and Gerald Davies had not been considered.
Later it was announced that Max Baise of Cape Town would
referee the match.

Thursday June 6

The Lions had their last hard session in readiness for the First
Test and looked quite good as critical South African eyes watched
them at work. The weather was perfect, warm and dry, but not
too hot. Cliff Morgan, Vivian and myself kicked and passed the
ball 'in touch' and Morgan's eyes were alight with pleasure as he
trotted over the famous Pretoria turf, the scene of his two triumphs
in 1955. The Springboks did not train but went to a golf course
for a 'walk round' and discussion with coach, Johan Claassens,
while Boy Louw was hovering in the background, full of ideas
and pleasant sayings. The Lions were entertained to lunch by the
Mayor of Pretoria at a delightful spot known as Fountains Kiosk,
and the excellent meal and good wine was much enjoyed by all, as
was the presentation of commemorative cuff-links to the British

visitors. The Pretoria officials were in good heart and mention must be made of Colonel A. F. Burger, Professor F. C. Eloff, Colonel P. Goossen, Secretary de W. Hoek and Chief Liaison officer, Hennie Nel. It was also good to chat about rugby round the world with former International Board member, Professor G. J. Potgieter, the tall man, who was dwarfed by Peter Stagg. Everyone was looking forward to the match and there were many callers at the hotel during the evening including Ralph Daniels, who has always helped the 'Welsh Press' on tour and Ted Cule, formerly of the Rhondda Valley but now busy with Iscor in Rhodesia. At this stage Telfer was still apparently fit and able to play, as was O'Shea, but a final decision had to be taken the following day.

Friday June 7

The tension of the impending test match began to reveal itself both in the city and in the two teams' hotels. Officials at the *Pretoria news* fixed up airmail pictures for the *Western Mail and Echo,* and the necessary shopping was done in warm sunshine. It was healthy weather and South Africans from all over the Republic poured into the administrative centre. Hundreds came from Rhodesia including Air-vice Marshall Harold Hawkins and the 'terrible twins', Freddie Dawe and George Pitt.

A letter was received from the former Glamorgan cricket captain, Trevor Arnott, wishing the Lions well in the test, and with Vivian and Cliff, I attended the cocktail party for former Springboks. It was most enjoyable and there was pleasure in meeting many great former players who had brought honour to their country's rugby, while the members of the 1951 and 1955 sides were delighted to see Cliff Morgan. His antics found Basie Vivers doubled up with laughter, while the organiser, Salty du Rand, thoroughly enjoyed himself. Dr Van Druten welcomed former players and visitors and I enjoyed discussing the game with Daan Retief, a fine back-row forward of 1955–56. The touring press presented a tankard to A. W. Retief, the retiring S.A. Board Liaison officer, and welcomed his successor Jack Horn, who was to prove a 'character' in the days that followed. Telfer withdrew during the afternoon and was replaced by Bob Taylor but the story was not released until the next morning.

Saturday June 8

One sensed the excitement early in the morning as the hotel
started rousing and everyone got down to the task in hand, for
there is something very special about the morning of a test match
in any country. Enthusiasts drive in early and the bars are full of
'experts' from the first moments of opening time, but on this morning everyone appeared to be racing for the Loftus Versveld
ground. Vivian and myself had a picnic lunch in the car park with
Malise Mackeurton and Derek Twigg and were fascinated by the
giant temporary stands and the long queues of spectators waiting
to enter. Later it was argued that there were not enough stewards
on duty and that it was difficult to move from the top of the stand
to the bottom, but these were teething troubles, since it was the
largest crowd ever housed at the ground. For the next test im-
provements will be made but on taking one's seat in the Press Box,
it looked an impressive sight and cameras clicked merrily to record
the occasion.

Conditions were perfect as the sun shone down from a blue
cloudless sky but there was a glare that tested the catchers of
high-kicks. The ground was hard, especially the cricket pitch, and
the Lions lost 25–20 in a match that was often exciting but never
great. The Springboks deserved their victory and could have won
by a larger margin; for the Lions it was a moment of truth. The
holiday was over; the battle was on! Du Preez, Naude and Visagie
were outstanding Springboks while Kiernan, McBride and Edwards
were brave Lions. Kiernan's wonderful place-kicking with six goals
in seven attempts was the best by a Lion in tests in South Africa.
He rose magnificently to the occasion, and but for the du Preez
try and Naude's second penalty, Kiernan would have won the
match for the Lions, against the run of play! Edwards finished
the match like a battered champion after a world title fight and
when he was injured late in the match, two first aid men asked
if they could do anything for him, and quickly came the reply,
'Yes, dig up the cricket pitch and bury me under it!' After the
match Danie Craven said, at the reception in a large marquee,
that it was one of the greatest tests he had seen. Here, for once,
the 'master' was surely carried away by the victory, for it was
not a great match, exciting in parts perhaps, but scrappy for long
periods, and punctuated by too many penalty kicks, correctly
awarded by Referee Max Baise, who did quite well, except per-

haps at the line-out where Stagg was subjected to some barging. The Lions did not impress tactically and the way ahead looked hard for them as they returned to their hotel for dinner. There was much noise during the night at the hotel and poor McBride slipped on the floor and became a 'casualty' with eight stitches in a leg and two in a finger. Thousands of words were cabled back to the British Sunday and Monday papers while South African papers in both languages gave high praise to the Springboks, which was deserved, and commented on the courage of the Lions. Courage, however, is never enough, for the Springboks had superior strength, team work and cohesive power. However, the turning point was the injury to Barry John, a major tragedy of the tour.

Sunday June 9

A day of rest for the battered Lions and Cliff Morgan and Dewi Griffiths did a TV interview with the Manager and Captain in the small hotel garden. However, it was not a 'Garden of Remembrance' and no one appeared sad. Everyone relaxed and Gareth Edwards, sporting a black eye and a body covered with bruises, come out shadow boxing, saying, 'Eddie told me to say nothing to the Press!' imitating another Welsh hero, Howard Winstone. Barry John sat in his room, writing letters, and doing his best to hide the bitter disappointment at suffering his injury. He told me, 'I was just starting to feel good in South Africa. I was determined to play my very best and to try and help the side win the series. Conditions are excellent for playing and I had never felt better. We had weathered the storm of the opening ten minutes and I felt we could run against them. If I do not get better quickly I intend going home before the end of the tour.' It was a bitter blow for both the player and the side and, I felt, John would have starred in the manner of Cliff Morgan and David Watkins, and maintained the high standard of Welsh outside-halves on tour. Most of the Lions were disappointed at not winning, but did not argue against the Springboks right to victory. John O'Shea said of opposing prop, Mof Myburg, 'He was really hard, but clean!' Another said, 'That was a fantastic try by du Preez!' David Brooks said, 'We were beaten by a better side, but it was our poorest display of the tour.' Ronnie Dawson criticised his team, and it is true they made tactical errors, but on reflection, they played only as well as they were allowed to do so. The main point of it all was that there was much work to be done on the training field, and in preparing the mental approach, as well as the calling up of a replacement. Many of the press visited the Country Club for lunch, the Harlequins Club for tea, and a large private house for an excellent braivelais dinner. Morgan and Griffiths, like Layton and Johnstone in the 1920's, provided entertainment and the host's family sang delightfully.

Monday June 10

There was a race to the airport early in the morning, but fortunately the Lions were late as well and the plane to Upington was delayed. I drove the car at a speed much faster than the limit and Vivian made hurried checks as to the correct route. It is unfair, perhaps, to criticise South African roads for it is such a big country and maintenance costs are high, but there is a desperate need for more sign-posts, especially in and out of major towns. One is really driving 'in the dark' as a stranger during the day, and by night it is almost impossible. Even the taxi-drivers are 'foxed' at night! Once in the plane, with Vivian providing South African champagne as a 'lift' for the day, we got to know our new liaison officer, Jack Horn, much better. This enlivened the journey and after touching down at Bloemfontein and Kimberley, we were greeted by a large and happy gathering at Upington. It was the first occasion for an International side to visit the town, although Cardiff was there in 1967. It will not be the last.

From the first moment, the Lions enjoyed themselves despite the cold and 'Little Jack Horner' led the party in a series of amusing activities, with perhaps the braivelais at the home of Owen and Anita Davies, the best of the visit. Jack Horn and Mayor Josling were on a par, as the most entertaining characters, for while Jack was an M.C. in the manner of Oliver Hardy, the Mayor did a wonderful imitation of the bagpipes. The Lions and other guests ate enormous plates of meat and vegetables, washed down with 'kroeg', and then sang lustily with other guests accompanied by – guess who – Morgan and Griffiths. This was one of the outstanding private parties of the tour, and it wafted away the atmosphere of disappointment created by the defeat in the test. A pleasant day indeed, fittingly concluded when we saw the Russian satellite in orbit from the farm lawns, as it whizzed past a beautifully bright full moon. The press gang was uniformly delighted; in all countries, nothing disarms more readily the pen of criticism than good friends, good food, good wine and, of course, good weather!

Tuesday June 11

This was the coldest day since the start of the tour with a biting wind and after the clouds banked themselves over the Town it started raining at lunch time and continued for most of the afternoon. The Lions party felt as cold as the coloured people and the walk to the post office, with afternoon cables, was unpleasant. This was the first rain since Stilfontein and it was cold stuff. The question of a replacement was on and off and Manager Brooks asked the South African Board for permission to approach the Four Home Unions officially. It was a matter of protocol to ask the Board, but they were not to give approval until two days later when the Lions reached Windhoek.

The generous North Western Cape Union gave a reception for the touring Press and it was attended by the local council and other dignatories. Cliff Morgan, Pat Marshall and Gert Kotze spoke in reply to the jolly Mayor's speech. During the evening several of the British press and TV party visited the lovely home of former Springbok Willelm Barnard (1949–52) who wanted to return some of the hospitality he had enjoyed in the British Isles. This is true of so many Springboks but especially the 1951–52 side, justly regarded as the best Springbok team to leave South Africa in the post war years. Willelm has a couple of farms and a transport business and he told me that he was concentrating more on producing beef, than Karakul lambs for their skins. As he said, so wisely, 'We have got to move with the times. South Africans are big beef-eaters, but they are demanding better quality. Thus I am experimenting with different breeds.' In one corner of his house were souvenirs of the 1951–52 tour including the ball used in the match against Newport, when Hennie Muller played so well.

Wednesday June 12

Another match day – this time *v.* North Western Cape Districts – and the town was soon alive with incoming traffic. The hotel filled quickly and Jack Horn said, 'This is the day we have been waiting for, the first international match at Upington.'

For the first time in South Africa a press liaison officer, in Peter Head, was in charge of the touring press and we were well looked after. However, Peter could not warm the atmosphere and it was really cold at the ground, although the sun was out and the sky pleasantly blue. In the curtain raiser, Springbok fly-half Piet Visagie was playing for his Club, Amazol, and did quite well against the local combined clubs. The Lions found the North Westerns stern opposition until the final quarter of an hour, and it is fair to suggest that the final tally of 25–5 flattered the Lions more than a little. The forwards won reasonable possession but the backs again lacked rhythm and, what had started the tour as our main striking force, fell short of expectations. Gibson was not happy until the pressure was off in the closing stages and then he ran in for a try, but he was fast becoming a problem boy. Ronnie Dawson thought the side had more bite in it, but I disagreed. Then he suggested it was the narrow field and that is why the mid-field players turned back inside instead of letting the ball go to the wings. However, Cliff Morgan measured the field and confirmed it was normal size. I was far from happy with the display and as a realist I felt there was room for considerable improvement. Jim Telfer passed through the match without further injury but the luckless John Taylor suffered a bang on his shoulder and this again put him out for a few matches. Some players cannot avoid injury, however hard they play, and John was unlucky on this tour. During the morning training session for the other players, Maurice Richards pulled a hamstring and this put John, Jones, Davies, Jarrett and Richards, of the Welsh players, on the injured list, while Jeff Young played because he had to do so. There was still no news of the replacement and the evening was taken up with a reception, a long-winded but pleasant dinner in which few people reached the sweet course, and a dance. One of the Lions, dancing with an attractive partner, asked if he could escort her home, but she said no . . . 'I am Coloured' and showed her identity card. It was true, but as the player said, 'She would pass for a European, anywhere'.

Thursday June 13
Everyone was engaged in letter writing during the morning and

the Press got all their cables away before proceeding to the airport for the flight to Windhoek in South West Africa. The stay at Upington has been thoroughly enjoyed and at the airport there were many friends to wish the team *bon voyage,* not to mention Mayor Josling, the happiest mayor in Southern Africa, whose parting gift to each member of the party was a packet of delicious dried raisins, produced in Upington. The visit had helped publicise the town and future international sides will call there, if only to meet Mayor Josling and Jack Horn! The flight to Windhoek by Viscount plane was along the edge of the Kalahari and even in the strong sunlight it looked grim and forbidding, but roads were sighted, now and again, and small holdings, while the main road and railway trekked north to South West Africa. We landed at the new J. G. Strydom Airport where a few months earlier the giant SAA 707 had crashed to its doom soon after take off. However, Captain Young touched down perfectly. Although from a cabin window it looked extremely warm, the temperature was only 50 degrees F. when we disembarked. Frikkie du Toit, a Rothman's representative, met Vivian and myself and drove us along the thirty miles into town. There is much that is attractive about Windhoek and although the citizens are a mixture of German, South African and British, and three languages are spoken, it is a friendly city. Post office officials were quick to meet the demands of the touring press and good food was provided at the mayoral banquet, but like the Welsh, the South Africans have too many speakers at official functions! The night was the coldest experienced up to this time and the cry went up for extra blankets and hot water bottles. However, there were plenty of letters received, which were read and re-read, and it was interesting to read my son Gareth's criticism of the Lions in the Test, as an observer 6,000 miles away! There was a great deal of logic in what he said. He pointed out that selection is all important and it must be 'horses for courses'. How right he was!

Friday June 14

Despite the extremely cold night, the dawn broke warm and clear and the Lions were soon at training. Cliff Morgan and myself went shopping after the announcement that a replacement had been asked for and that it would be Ken Goodall, the Irish

Number eight. There was much discussion among the players –
although the team needed another back-row forward to make the
number six instead of five and redress the balance with 14 backs
(excluding John) and sixteen forwards, many wondered whether
he would stand up to the hard, hurly-burly of test rugby. Most
South Africans asked, 'Was there a bigger man available?' He
would leave London the next day and join the Lions party at
Johannesburg.

Windhoek is 5,428 feet above sea level and 990 miles from
Cape Town and is the principal business and sports centre of
the South West territory. Its population is approximately 25,000
Europeans and 18,000 Coloured and Bantu. It produces four
newspapers, one in English, two in Afrikaans and one in German.
The town is dominated by a circle of hills and at the summit of
three of the hills there are castles built in German medieval style,
plus a museum housed in a German fort (Alte Feste). One of the
most interesting national monuments is a little engine, coaches and
trucks that used to run between Walvis Bay, on the West coast,
and the German border near Swakopmund. Another interesting
item was the dress of the dignified native Herero women, which
consisted of a turban, a dress with a fitted bodice with leg o'
mutton sleeves, and a voluminous sweeping skirt, said to require
22 yards of material. This style had been handed down from the
wives of the early German missionaries. Windhoek is the centre
of the karakul skin industry and also of the big game hunting
safaris in the area. Manager Brooks and a party spent the afternoon hunting kudu, while the South West team had a final work-
out during the evening. Some of the team members had to make
a round trip of 800 miles to play which was indicative of their
enthusiasm.

Saturday June 15
    Yet another match day dawned warm and clear and the morn-
ing was taken up in purchasing skins for relatives and friends at
a reasonable price. Vivian engaged bookmakers and police riders
to ensure that he got his telex copy of the match report to the
Sunday Times, London, before deadline-time and he succeeded.
As a result he gave all of his 'team' a champagne supper which was
much appreciated. It speaks well of his ingenuity in arranging the
system, which earned him the names of 'Scoop Jenkins' and

'Deadline Viv'. The BBC 2 TV team did a good job of work, and we were entertained by the advice of Jumbo du Tronich, a refugee prop from Rhodesia, who helped all and sundry. The match *v.* South West Africa saw the Lions play well, while the S.W.A. captain spent all the afternoon chasing Gareth Edwards without success. After the work was done and the cables had been put to bed we had dinner, a few drinks, and then coffee by candlelight in a pleasant coffee-bar at the Windsor Café. Paul Irwin said it reminded him of *Journey's End* or a cellar in Munich! The service, and the coffee, was excellent, and fortunately the night was not as cold as anticipated.

Sunday June 16

There was much to do in the morning, for the Springbok team for the Second Test had to be commented upon, since the selectors had been forced to make one change as the excellent flank forward, Greyling, had broken a collar bone the previous day. His place was taken by Lourens of the Northern Transvaal. Despite the fact that the Lions were due to play the Transvaal on the Tuesday, Manager Brooks issued no team, and everyone awaited the vital decision on Gibson, who had not really regained his form. I suggested, once again, in an emergency, Edwards and Roger Young at half-back with Edwards at outside-half.

The Johannesburg-based camp-followers decided to return by the early plane, the 707 London-Cape Town plane, that was calling at Windhoek and due to leave there at mid-day. They got to the airport in time, but owing to technical trouble were delayed six hours, and so the Lions party and British press left them behind when their Viscount departed at 5.0 p.m. On board the 707 was replacement Ken Goodall. We met him but he was not allowed by Customs to change planes and so arrived after us at Johannesburg. On the way from the hotel to Windhoek Airport the Press coach was 'disturbed' by a fire extinguisher that fell from its position and scattered everyone with foam! The coach looked a shambles inside and on arrival at the airport, the Lions laughed and laughed, and the Press were forced to have a 'wash down' before take-off. David Frost tried to hook the extinguisher out of sight, and so sharp was his strike that the S.A. Referees Association would have blown for 'feet up'! The air trip was amusing with O'Shea in good form, and his description of a fashion parade was excellent though slightly embarrassing for the poor air hostess! At the Jan Smuts Airport, we were met by Walley Barnes, former captain of Arsenal and Wales, and now manager of the local Highland Park Club. It was good to chat to him about soccer and its growth in South Africa, and he believed there was a future for it. 'We need more good young players from England to really establish the game here, but they cost a lot of money,' he said. The Lions stayed at the New Skyline Hotel in the centre of the 'beatnik' district of Johannesburg at Hillbrow. However, we were all well-treated there and the manager and his wife, Mr and Mrs Keith Lamb from England, were much amused at the current report in the London *People*, hinting that the Lions were living like 'tramps'. Dick Beaumont (alias Ian Todd) didn't actually write 'tramps' but perhaps inferred it. Immediately David Brooks denied this, but the article actually developed as a result of a private discussion at Upington concerning whether the Lions were getting the best hotels on tour.

Monday June 17

A quick look at the 'Golden City' or 'concrete jungle' called 'Jowburg' by its inhabitants, revealed that it was still growing apace with more sky-scrapers, more one way streets to deal with its ever increasing traffic and dearer taxi fares. It was pleasant to visit Ellis Park again and to see the new 'Glasshouse'. Jeppe van Heerden was in great form, and as busy as ever, but I missed many familiar faces who had been 'lost' in the administrative 'take over' of a few years previously. The Transvaal Union in recent years appears to have become rather anti-press and this is sad, for the Johannesburg papers are generous in their coverage of the game. Maybe there are faults on both sides but the banning of Gert Koetze, sports Editor of the *Die Vaderland*, because of an article he wrote, did not appear to be a particularly wise move. An experienced rugby writer, Gert had to spend the next day playing golf instead of watching the Transvaal beat the Lions. The Lions announced their team and although it was the morning 'papers turn to have it there was no 'embargo' for 'Spontaneous Sam' and S.A.P.A. distributed it immediately. However during the afternoon, one person who shall remain nameless and was in no way connected with the Lions party or the official press party, played a very 'sick' joke on Sam Merwis, a particularly happy and helpful colleague. His office rang the hotel and the room occupied by the Transvaal Union asking for Sam, and someone answered, 'He's gone to hospital with a heart attack'. It just wasn't funny and the worry and distress it caused, is easily imagined. Investigations were made and suspects confirmed but no one admitted the error and apologised at the time. Later a general half-hearted apology was made but it took Sam a long time to get over it. A good practical joke is amusing, but this was 'sick' humour. During the evening the full Lions party attended an excellent theatre show, *Strike it Rich*, as the guests of the Mayor, and this was one of the most entertaining official evenings of the tour.

Tuesday June 18

It was match day again and during the morning, Gareth Edwards was withdrawn from the Lions team in case of possible injury before the test, and McBride had to stand down because of a festering finger. This weakened the Lions but they still could have won the match against Transvaal. They lost because they did not take their first-half chances after holding an early six-nil lead. In the second half the referee, Mr Stander, in my opinion penalised the Lions rather harshly and both Roger Young at scrum-half and John Pullin as hooker were in trouble. The Lions could not break down a good Transvaal defence and their opponents played it tight, with scrum-half Vos kicking continually. There was a big banquet in the 'Glasshouse' later, which looked more like a spacious 'dance and gin palace' than a real rugby meeting house despite the liberal hospitality. As one official said 'We are becoming more of an entertaining union than a rugby union.' He could have been right, but this appears to be a modern trend in rugby football nowadays. Still, the Transvaal had beaten the Lions for the first time since the War and it was also the Lions first defeat on the famous Ellis Park since 1938. A sad day and not a particularly happy match, although the Transvaal deserved their victory. Later there were accusations in the local press that the 'Lions had sworn at their opponents on the field'. How 'terrible' this was, and many a former player laughed and laughed! This match marked the halfway stage of the tour with ten matches played, eight won and two lost. Soon there would be a drawn match!

Wednesday June 19

Early the next day the rugby caravan moved on and the Lions were airborne early for Port Elizabeth in a 727 plane. The coach ride to the airport was one of the fastest rides experienced in South Africa and even the 'veteran' campaigner, Vivian was frightened enough to ask the driver to slow down. As Clifford M. said, 'Even Phil Davies would have failed to get through that gap,' as the coach sliced between two cars in separate lanes. There's only the quick and the dead on South African roads, and there was more danger on the roads than in the air on this morning. The Marine Hotel welcomed us and I shared a room with Paul Irwin, facing the sea.

A remarkable raconteur, Paul kept me amused during our stay and the setting and service at the hotel, plus the willingness of liaison officer, Jimmy Ward, and his helpers, certainly put our status far above that of 'tramps'! The Lions trained during the afternoon and the Test XV played in red jerseys, so that the morning 'paper men were able to forecast it, although it was not announced until the next morning. Keri Jones was on the wing and Edwards at scrum-half but no Welshmen among the forwards. This caused raised eyebrows from the Springbok press and they asked, where is Delme Thomas, and what about Gerald Davies in the centre? It was a little puzzling but Jones withdrew later because he was not happy about his ham-string injury and Hinshelwood took his place. This left only one Welshman in the side, and the smallest contribution by Wales to any Lions test team since the war. The cables hummed merrily as they were despatched to all countries. Who was to be the referee for the Second Test? That was a good question, but we had to wait for the next day for this one, although a friendly PE official whispered in my ear, 'Mr Schoeman'. I was perturbed but kept the silence of confidence. It was late at night and tongues generally talk more freely at this hour, but I realised that it was to set-off a chain re-action the next day. There was trouble brewing!

Thursday June 20

This was an important day, for at the press conference to announce the Test XV Manager Brooks related the details of the appointment of Mr Schoeman as referee. Before the Press Conference he discussed the situation with Vivian and myself and he

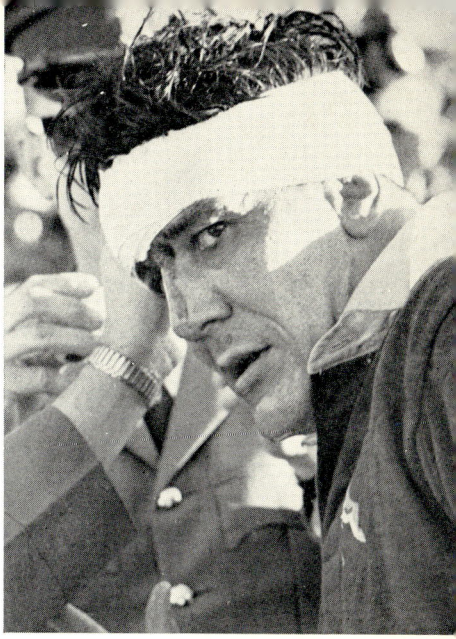

PLATE 15. *Above, left:* Lions lock Willie McBride gets up high to beat Tiny Naude to the ball in the Second Test. PLATE 16. *Above, right:* Injured Springbok lock, Frik du Preez, watches the progress of the Second Test as he has his head bandaged on the side-line. PLATE 17. *Below:* Jim Telfer, the Lions number eight and pack leader, gathers from a maul as he is challenged by Lourens (*left*) and de Villiers in the Second Test at Port Elizabeth

PLATE 18. The Second Test. *Top:* A ruck is formed after Telfer goes down (he is on ground) and Horton (centre) goes in search of the ball. PLATE 19. *Below:* Horton emerges with the ball and gets it away to Edwards as Telfer watches anxiously

wanted to read out a long statement on the activity behind the scenes, but we suggested a straight-forward statement. This was read out and stated that the Lions had asked for a referee outside the panel of four nominated, and he was Mr Walter Lane of Natal. The South African Board did not want Mr Lane and said that he was not even a reserve for the panel, and they appointed a sixth referee, Mr Schoeman of the Western Province, who had had charge of the Lions match at Upington. It had been agreed at the start of the tour that the Lions could ask for a referee from outside the panel, but that if he was not acceptable to the Board they would appoint another referee not on the panel that had to be accepted by the Lions. It was a case of South Africa really having a referee of which they thoroughly approved, but the Four Home Unions had agreed to the policy and that was that. Naturally this was 'news' and the Second Test got off to a sensational start. Later in the day, Doctor Danie Craven, central figure in the happenings and in the controversy that was to follow, was quizzed by Vivian, Cliff and myself, on the laws and referees, and he emphasised that the 'Board would never have Lane, for he is not ninth reserve'. Yet I did point out that the Board's agreement was tantamount to a veto in power, and that in the British Isles a South African team has the choice of nine referees, all NEUTRAL for a test. I feel the Board could have allowed Mr Lane to have charge of the test and met the Lions request, although they were quite in order to carry out to the letter, paragraph EA2 of the Tour agreement. However, it was to raise a controversy that reverberated round the world. In the end I am sure the Board wished they had appointed Mr Lane.

Friday June 21

The main eve-of-the-match comment concerned the appointment of the Referee, and newspapers at home and abroad gave it a 'good show'. Barry John was examined by a medical panel of three doctors and they indicated that he could train in ten days time and perhaps, with good fortune, play in the final three matches of the tour. He was delighted with the news and agreed to stay on, subject to South African Board approval. John told me, 'I am delighted that such a decision has been made as I have now something to work for. I would love to play again in South Africa before I leave and my shoulder is much easier.' He rang

his home in West Wales and passed the news on that he was staying with the team and all his colleagues appeared pleased, and
especially Gareth Edwards and Mike Gibson. Most Afrikaans
papers asked why Gerald Davies and Delme Thomas had been
omitted and as a Welshman, I was asked whether I was in agreement with only one Welsh player being included in the Test XV.
The answer was simple enough . . . It is a British team and it
deserves the support of all Britishers. As to its technical com-
petence, that would be known only after the match, and any valid
criticism of the selectors would have to be made then. Edwards
was asked by a pressman if he felt lonely as the only Welshman
in the side and he replied, quickly, 'I have not thought about it!'
The Springboks held a re-union and the Lions packed parcels to
send home. Kiernan was quietly confident that the team was
stronger and had a 'fifty-fifty' chance of success. However, the
Springboks would start as favourites on the morrow, but one felt
that the Lions would give them a harder match. The BBC 2 Film
Unit received their first 'masterpiece' from London by air, the
colour film of the 1st Test and both teams watched it. It was
quite impressive and proved that the Springboks were the better
side at Pretoria. Would they be as impressive the next day? Paul
Irwin looked into his 'crystal ball' and found that the Springboks
were rather complacent.

Saturday June 22

This was a day to remember and one of those days on tour
when the atmosphere is charged with rumour and counter rumour,
and press men feed like hungry vultures upon the actions on the
field and the sayings about it. No touring pressman from either
country could grumble at the 'menu' on this day when the Lions
shared a hard and sternly fought draw with the Springboks at the
Boete Erazmus Stadium. Several things were noticeable from the
Press Box; first that a Springbok forward spent most of
the match double-banking near the front of the line-out; secondly
that Pullin appeared reluctant to strike in the set-scrums
and Edwards could not satisfy the referee while putting the ball
in. Finally, Gibson was deliberately punched while he was
pinioned in a loose maul. Fortunately this was the only 'fighting'
incident of the match which was hard throughout but mainly
clean. The Lions defended superbly to earn their draw, but the

Referee's interpretations did not impress them and immediately after the match, Manager Brooks said, 'we were most disappointed with the standard of refereeing and thought the fact that a Springbok forward could double-bank continuously at the line-out was disgraceful'. We used this in our cables and as we were typing, Mr du Toit, the chairman of the South African Association of Referees, came to the Press Box and he was asked about the 'alleged' double-banking. 'I didn't see any,' he said. At the after-the-match function, Danie Craven anticipated trouble from the Press in a diplomatic speech. The Lions had prepared a 'good' speech for Tom Kiernan, but he was not asked to speak, as were the captains at Pretoria. One sensed that a 'storm' was breaking and Manager Brooks poured out his heart to me at dinner in the hotel. 'We haven't got a chance' he said, 'in the remaining two tests because they will not let us win the ball'. He went on to relate that he had visited Mr Schoeman before the start of the match to chat with him and found that he had been warned to the effect that the Lions front-row had to be watched, also the scrum-half. This greatly disturbed Brooks, who felt if all referees were so warned the Lions had no chance. 'Pullin is one of fairest hookers in the British Isles,' added Brooks, 'and the players had a hard time of it on the field.' It was all so sad and I was sorry for Brooks at this stage, for although the team had shown remarkable courage in gaining the draw there was little apparent hope for the future. The team went dancing and several celebrated but the controversy grew as midnight was reached and the pop of champagne corks echoed through the players' room. It had been a rugby day to remember and the Sunday papers were out on the streets of London with their hard-hitting cables.

Sunday June 23

This was the morning after the night before, the typewriters clicking merrily as cables were prepared for the 'papers of the rival countries. Springbok critics could not understand why the match had been drawn, for they felt their side had enough chances to have won by ten points. They were uncertain about the refereeing but felt that Brooks should have taken a member of the panel when Lane was refused. Brooks gave interviews to South African pressmen and Paul Irwin prepared a powerful piece on 'Rugby Volcanoes' before we left by air for Johannesburg. It was

sad to leave P.E. where we had received excellent treatment from
local officials and the hotel staff and no one could say there had
been a 'shortage' of copy. It had been a real news week-end, if a
sad one.

After arriving safely at Johannesburg following some whistle-
stops at East London and Bloemfontein, the 727 landed perfectly
at Jan Smuts Airport. The Lions checked in at the New Skyline
Hotel, where a warm welcome awaited them, before setting off by
train to Nelspruit and the Kruger National Park. Some members
of the Press party accompanied them; some went to Laurenço
Marques and others remained at the New Skyline (Viv, Cliff and
myself) in an effort to get up to date with the 'admin' and our
books. There is comparatively little time on a long tour to rest and
relax and get everything up-to-date, week by week, for so much
time is taking in studying players, checking activities, meeting
officials, attending practices and press conferences, eating, occasionally drinking, writing letters and cards and, most important of
all, preparing cables for transmission and 'getting them to the post
office on time'. As Cliff Morgan remarked half-way through this
tour, 'It is far easier being a player than a press correspondent'. He
should know by now.

Monday June 24

The morning papers contained reports of the British pressmen
on the Second Test and referee 'troubles', in abbreviated form. The
'wicked' British press had been at it and their comments were the
talk of the Republic. Terry O'Connor (*Daily Mail*) and Ian Todd
(*Sun*) had suggested that the Lions should go home in protest
against the refereeing! All had requested that something should
be done. The South African morning papers continued the 'Saga'.
More cables flashed away to London and the air was full of
strange comments, allegations and denials. During the evening
the four travelling Welshmen tasted real sophisticated South
African hospitality at Sandhurst.

One of the number, tired by the heavy duties of the tour, had a
short nap, but the host and hostess, Malise and Joan Mackeurtan,
made sure every visitor and neighbour thoroughly enjoyed the show.

Tuesday June 25

The morning papers contained more 'stirring' comment on the

Lions who were now 'in dispute' with South African referees. In his absence in the Game Reserve, one Afrikaans paper stated that Manager Brooks was the real cause of the dispute. Former Springboks rallied to the side of the referee. Danie Craven said the critics should not write in condemnation of referees when they did not know the laws themselves. Referee Schoeman was quoted, giving the reasons why he penalised Pullin in the Test: the infringements included 'hanging', 'swinging', 'lowering and not binding', 'having no pushing foot' and 'moving to the mouth of the tunnel'. As they used to say in the barrack rooms during the War, 'Schoeman threw the book at him!', and poor Pullin, a well-known, fair and upright hooker was in temporary 'disgrace'. Next came the inspired suggestion that a new panel would be offered for the Third Test (this did not materialise). I wrote in the Argus Group that the battle of words should cease forthwith and all parties get together, as Mr Wilson would say, round the table and sort out their many problems. I suggested that the S.A. Board should state in writing what they wanted and then ask the Lions to abide by the request. It would be so much easier! We had lunch with the General Manager of the Standard Bank of South Africa, George Oxford, and two executives and they, like true South Africans, wanted to see the dispute ended quickly. The team were still in the Game Reserve, and International Board members, Alf Wilson and Kobus Louw, were there too, with their wives, and like rugby men, they must have talked of many things. Of laws, referees, tours, teams and managers, and the Press!

Wednesday June 26

Danie Craven was annoyed today at various statements attributed to him and he appealed for everyone to get on with the job of making the tour a success. He felt certain members of the Press were trying to stir up trouble, but the majority of the travelling press had only repeated the complaints of the Lions, who were genuinely distressed. However, there were exceptions in each country! No cables were sent today and I moved on with the book and the many letters to be answered. Slowly things got up-to-date and during the evening Viv, Dewi and myself visited the lovely home of Morag and Ralph Daniel, who have a magnificent collection of sea stones and shells plus many a deep sea fishing trophy. His relatives and friends proved excellent company and we were able to relax in the quiet atmosphere with good food and wine.

Thursday June 27

The Lions returned from the Game Reserve this morning and again took up residence in the New Skyline. Local pressmen met Manager Brooks at the station but he was restrained and non-communicative. Something was afoot! He was cautious now and the audacity of Port Elizabeth had disappeared. In his wisdom, he held a press conference in the early afternoon for eighteen press-men but having given the team for the Eastern Transvaal match, then said, 'I have nothing further to say on the referees dispute, but if I do have anything to say, it will be said to the South African Board'. The South African Press regarded this as soft-peddling, and suggested that Brooks had been 'gagged'. The two Scottish International Board members were staying at the hotel but refused to be drawn. Poor Alf Wilson, with whom I had travelled in 1959 to the Antipodes, broke his thumb coming back from the Game Reserve and he was heavily bandaged but remained cheerful! During the evening we visited the home of likeable Jeppe Van Heerden and his family and he told us much about the method of distributing 65,000 Test tickets for the 4th Test. There is no direct distribution to clubs as in the British Isles, and this means much more work.

Friday June 28

This was D-Day as far as the referees dispute was concerned, for the South African Board decided to meet during the evening in Johannesburg and discuss the situation with the Lions manage-ment, David Brooks and Ronnie Dawson. It was to be the big meeting, and it was, for no punches were pulled, so I am told, and there was a great deal of straight talking on both sides. There were accusations and denials by both sides. It was a lively meeting al-though no details of the discussion were given to the Press – only a straightforward statement. I was given the details, in confidence, but it is no good repeating them because it would serve no purpose, and the British management just had to abide by the decisions taken. I think they were unhappy at first but their temper and enthusiasm changed after the memorable victory at Pretoria, a few days later, and their thoughts on referees were turned in another direction after the 'Battle of Springs', which was to follow the next day. At 10 p.m. the following statement was issued on behalf of the meeting by the 'peacemaker', my good friend Kobus Louw, who is always the complete rugby diplomat. It read; 'A joint meeting between the management of the British Touring team, Messrs, D. K. Brooks and A. R. Dawson, the Executive, and the Laws Committee of the South African Board, was held in Jo'burg on Friday June 28th. Various matters concerning the tour were discussed in detail and all difficulties resolved, apart from the interpretations of the laws, on which agreement was reached, and particular reference was made to: (a) regarding the suggestion that the Lions have been accused of complaining about the standard of referees and refereeing; the Lions management wish to state categorically, that at no time have they complained, officially, whether they have lost or won. (b) In respect of the much-publicised allegation that Doctor Craven had instructed or influenced referees, which might have been to the detriment of the Lions, it is emphatically denied and this accepted by all'. So that was that, the Lions management had made the peace; there was little else they could do!

Saturday June 29

If one had thought there had been controversy before this day, then all were in for a big shock. This was O'Shea day in the 'Battle of Springs', but it started so well. A very pleasant drive to Springs with excellent banter on the way, with Malise and his many charming friends, was climaxed by an excellent picnic lunch. It was just like 'Twickers' except that the illustrious 'Wakers' was not there to taste the 'champers'! There were however, other, more delectable compensations. A South African backed into Vivian's car as he was parking, and at first refused to exchange addresses, but seeing there were so many witnesses, most of them charming, he had to do so! The police did not appear too concerned! After a lunch of rare quality with Joan as hostess, all the party proceeded to the Stand and the pitch looked really hard, a strange yellow colour produced by the hard frosts of winter, and the raised cricket square in the centre, looked even harder. The match against Eastern Transvaal was the first since the Second Test and obviously the referee was 'on the spot'. An old friend of many years, Bert Woolley, was the man in charge and he came to the Press Box to greet me before the kick-off and to talk about his visit to Wales as manager of the

Transvaal High Schools team in the 1950's. I wished him luck, little realising that he would soon be holding the 'rugby baby', but he must be exonerated for there was little else he could do. John O'Shea was provoked as one scrum broke up in the second half, following a series of small incidents and meleés in which blows were struck, and he chased away to 'clobber' the offender. He swung fists in the open and was spotted by Referee Woolley who had to stop him and then send him from the field. This was sad indeed, for O'Shea had been unlucky, while the provoker got away 'scot free'. Referee Woolley had done what he thought to be right at the time, and I admired his having the courage of his convictions. Kiernan echoed this in public later in the day.

However, this was only the start of the rugby 'shindig', the like of which I have not seen since an elderly lady hit Wilfred Wooller with an umbrella after he had won the match for Cardiff on one of the more historic Welsh grounds! O'Shea was pelted with oranges and cushions and other articles as he walked from the touch-line to the mouth of the tunnel, and Ronnie Dawson and Horton escorted him there in face of the show of 'anger'. Suddenly a spectator rushed out and struck O'Shea full in the face! This blow lit the blue touch-paper of the fuse of fury, and in less time than it takes to say 'John O'Shea' there was a heaving, mauling mass of spectators, Lions non-players, officials, friends and police engaged in the hottest maul of the tour. The game went on gaily, but the press and TV cameras were riveted on the all action, all-in wrestling-cum-boxing contest that was going on at the mouth of the tunnel. The best punch was landed by 'little' Willie John McBride, who struck the offending spectator with a right cross, and followed with a left, before the police restored comparative order. The offending spectator had his spectacles broken and was cut about the face; later he and his friend were arrested.

Order was restored and we all went back to watching the game again, but although the Lions produced some of their best running rugby, it was the 'scenes' that filled the many cables pouring out of telegraph office below the stand for home and foreign consumption. The Press worked away madly at the match. Everyone thought it was the first occasion for a Lion to be sent off, but I remembered the late Rhys Gabe telling me that one of his team mates had been sent off in Australia in 1904, and that the players had tried to persuade the referee to let him come back on to the field after the interval. He did not, but the Rugby Union exonerated the unlucky player, David Dobson of England. His offence: 'Making an obscene remark to the referee!

The journey back to Springs in the dark was made difficult by the lack of signposts, a common feature of travel in the Republic, but Dewi managed the journey well, although the driving of three cars abreast, at times, by South African drivers, caused us to wish we were in the maul at Springs. It appeared so much safer!

O'Shea took the decision well and the team supported him gaily. Kiernan said at the after-match reception that he admired the courage of the referee, even if not all the Lions agreed with his decision. The Prime Minister, Mr John Vorster, was at the match and the reception and I was delighted at his reluctance to seek the limelight, and to make a speech. Quite different from one leader, I know! Late in the evening, as Viv and I were having a coffee before going to bed, David Brooks visited us, and poured out his heart concerning the 'troubles', but again he spoke 'in confidence'. He was sad and a little depressed. Was there any more trouble to come? The approach of Wednesday's hard match against the Northern Transvaal did not help matters.

Sunday June 30

Most of Sunday was spent working and typing. There was so much to do! Cables, articles, interviews, letters and record-keeping held one's attention until nearly dinner time, and then an 'invasion' party headed by Vivian, and guided by Malise, set off for Sandhurst to forget the troubles for a couple of hours. There were counter-troubles there but most people enjoyed them, and Rosebud became patron-in-chief to the Welsh Glee Club, while Cliff Morgan said it was the first time he had ever broken a finger playing the piano!

Monday July 1

Before breakfast John O'Shea was 'tried' and reprimanded, but reinstated! It was the earliest 'hearing' in the history of rugby football, and a hurried statement, typed out in Cliff Morgan's room at the dictation of Jack Horn, made reference to the crowd's behaviour and the 'visited' Union. The sub-committee hearing the case consisted of Dr. Frank Mynhardt (President E.T.R.U.), Mr Gert Mollett (Vice-president of the E.T.R.U.) and David Brooks.

D

They did not discuss the case for any great length of time, although I understand it was first suggested O'Shea received a one-match suspension. and then a 'severe' reprimand, but Brooks resisted. Eventually there was full agreement on a straight reprimand with immediate 're-instatement'. A light and friendly decision – with the punishment really fitting the crime!

Everyone in the Lions party was delighted, especially John O'Shea who had apologised to the referee, and refused to prefer charges against the irate spectator. He was happy, and so were the rugby men of Cardiff and Wales! The referee had awakened me from a deep slumber at 7.0. a.m., before the hearing, to say how sorry he was about the incident, but that he had no option at the time. I agreed with him, but then I realised that his report was likely to help O'Shea. It did, and Referee Woolley lost no friends by his reasonable action. He, too, like O'Shea. would continue happily in the game. When we arrived at Pretoria, Manager Brooks announced that O'Shea would play on Wednesday against the Northern Transvaal and this caused Paul Irwin to comment, 'It reminds me of the war. As soon as a pilot is shot down and rescued; send him up again'! I was worried lest O'Shea be 'put upon' and not feel able to retaliate, but the Northerns made no threats. Their captain, former Springbok Piet Uys, was a gentleman in his approach, and he would have no nonsense, even from his powerful 'jumbo' sized pack, which was as good, in the opinion of the locals, as any test side fielded by South Africa. The days were warm at Pretoria but the nights cold, and the Assembly Hotel, though doing everything possible for us, was not able to change to central heating at the drop of a hat. Extra blankets were provided but it was still cold.

For the Lions this was another sad day, for an x-ray examination of Ken Goodall's hand, injured at Springs, revealed that it was broken in three places and that he would not play again on the tour. He had arrived on June 16th and was out of action on July 1; a tragedy indeed for such a promising young player. Goodall played most of the Eastern Transvaal match with his hand damaged and in pain and this one and only performance by him suggested that he would have proved an asset to the side. The cables flashed to London but no official statement was made by the Management until the next day. Now, at last, the equally unlucky Bryan West would get his chance!

Tuesday July 2

David Brooks announced today that Goodall would not play again on the tour, but would return home after the Third Test. Permission had been requested from the South African Board to send for a replacement, and at the same time a cable was sent to the Four Home Unions requesting that West's fitness be checked. This meant 'if fit, will travel', and later in the week it was announced from London that West would leave to join the party on Sunday at Cape Town. On this day Jim Telfer visited a specialist at Pretoria to check on his knee, which was knocked in training the previous day. He was advised to rest it, but Telfer was determined to play in the 'Fifth Test' against the powerful Northerns and did not withdraw from the chosen side. Millar and McBride were not available and so it was going to be a real test for the Lions.

The evening was spent at a pleasant restaurant by Viv and myself as the guests of Ted Cule, a former Welshman now resident in Rhodesia. The discussion was interesting and the arguments put forward for Rhodesia, most valid, while everyone there was grateful for the Lions visit. The joke of the day was related by Cliff Morgan who said, 'I have had a request from Frik du Preez to put a hood over the cameras during the match, so the TV would not record him hitting anyone!' Even Frik laughed when Cliff told him the story, just before the kick-off on the next day.

Wednesday July 3

Yet another interesting match day that dawned perfectly. Soon the hotel was 'invaded'. the best of the invaders being our many friends from Johannesburg. With Joan and Malise Mackeurton and their most interesting friends, Vivian, Cliff and myself had another extremely amusing picnic lunch. This was a splendid first hour to a happy day, for the Lions produced their 'Greatest Hour' of the tour. In fact, they found themselves, for with a remarkable recovery, they beat the Northerns against all the odds, after being 13–5 down in the middle of the first half.

It was *the* match of the tour, and it restored the game in South Africa to its proper place after a temporary lapse, and won back the affection of followers in the Republic for the Lions. The referees' dispute was forgotten and O'Shea was allowed to lead the Lions in to the dressing rooms at the end of the match – and thus

even Springs was forgotten. It is easy to imagine the celebrations
that followed!

This was a big night in every sense of the word. Vivian decide
to give a dinner party to all our friends from Johannesburg, and
ordered French champagne. It cost £6 a bottle, so the four Welsh
hosts 'bought' the hotel when the bills were paid early the next
morning while the expense accounts went four weeks into the
red! But what an enjoyable party it was; one of the best of the
many we have attended or given on six tours. Ralph Daniel
did a Zulu dance; Jack Horn won a prize for modern ballroom
dancing; Cliff and Dewi set up a new record for non-stop piano
playing, the natives employed by the hotel did a dance, while the
Welsh Glee Club, under the eyes of its president, sang the top
'Blues' number, *Birth of the Blues*, Paul Irwin sang *Underneath the
Arches*, and Chick Henderson did a lot of damage to *Old Man
River!* Lee got lost in a curtain and the party ended at 1.0 a.m.
with the revellers disappearing in the night and Johannesburg. The Lions sang well through the night and the tour was happy
and alive again. It was a touch of 1955 and this by any standards,
was extremely pleasing. Now the target was the Third Test and at
least a share of the rubber. Yet there was sadness, too, for poor Jim
Telfer, who had further damaged his knee in the match. Yet he
was a hero, make no mistake about it, for he had to leave the field
after receiving a kick in the head which required stitches over each
eye, We thought he would not return and Delme Thomas went
down to change, but Telfer returned. He whipped his forwards
for the final effort and when it was all over; aching and damaged,
but splendidly happy, he told me, 'That was the greatest victory in
any match I have played. It was wonderful to play in, and the lads
were superb!' Scotsmen do not wear their hearts on their sleeves,
but Telfer was a brave Scot on this day.

Thursday July 4

There was a bad start to the day; an early morning take-off
from Jan Smuts Airport for Kimberley via Bloemfontein. Such
starts are never popular on tour, and as the Viscount was 'dry',
no one could have nip of the dog that had so thoroughly bitten
them the night before! We saw Doctor Craven at Bloemfontein
and David Brooks, Cliff, Barry John and Ken Goodall went with
him to study methods and organisation for the Craven week. It was

being staged in the City and 350 selected schoolboys from all over
South Africa had a week's coaching from 25 former Springboks,
and a series of matches. All were impressed with what they saw
and the four Lions were 'awarded' their Craven caps. This has
been done in Wales on a smaller scale for the past five years at
Aberystwyth and is of inestimable value.

Jack Horn was appointed temporary honorary acting unpaid
manager until the return of Brooks later in the day and Kimberley
gave the team a good welcome. Bryan West had been requested
as a replacement but there was still no announcement from London.
Most of the party went to the 'drive-in' cinema to see that excellent
film, the *Deadly Affair*, but the Welsh revellers retired early!
There was peace again in the Lions Camp and the tour was back
on the rails, suggesting an exciting final stage.

Friday July 5

If we thought it had been cold in Pretoria at night, it REALLY
was cold at Kimberley! We had one bar electric fires in the rooms
but the drop in temperature was considerable. Also, they must
do more railway shunting at night in Kimberley than at Severn
Tunnel Junction. I used to love steam engines but they made one
h . . . of a noise at Kimberley. However, it is a friendly town and
I placed a few rand for the Press Gang on the Durban 'July' Race
with rather disastrous results. It would appear that the 'Four
Fizzers', as the four Welshmen were christened (being a more
modern group than the Glee Club), have little knowledge of horse
flesh! Even the hot favourite did not win the race the next day,
while our 'special', Blue Tarvenier, couldn't stand the pace.

It was good to walk round the streets of Kimberley again after
an interval of 13 years. The town had changed considerably. The
biggest 'man made hole' in the world was still there, of course,
and was duly inspected. Kimberley has an altitude of over
4,000 ft., is over 600 miles from Cape Town, and is the centre
of the diamond industry. It boasts a newspaper with the most
fascinating title of all, *The Diamond Fields Advertiser*, and you
can almost see Barney Barnato buying his way into the Kimberley
Club. What great, exciting times they must have been in those
early days from 1871 onwards. It is said that the irregularity of
the roads in the town (or should I say City) is a legacy from the
times when the 'roads zigzagged among the diggings'. Perhaps

the most interesting place to visit in the City is the Duggan Cronin
Bantu Gallery was has nearly 4,000 pictorial studies of Bantu
tribal life and custom. Kimberley is the headquarters of the
Griquas Union which has a fine record against touring teams.
The captain for the morrow was the well-known threequarter,
Francois Roux, who is as gentle off the field as he is hard-hitting
on it. What he, and we, did not know, was that he was to win
back his place in the Springbok side for defending sternly against
the Lions in this game.

Saturday July 6

Another match day and a sunny but cold one. It was notable
on tour as being the last day in office, as the Board's representative, of Jack 'Will Fly' Horn. It was as sad for him as it
was for us, and he much enjoyed the presentation, on the previous
evening, of a tankard from the travelling press. It was rather a
good party, with some fast drinking, and one felt at the time,
that of all the 'big' press parties (in numbers I mean) this was
one of the happiest. I can recall no dispute between any of them
that was ever taken seriously, and this is a tribute to the spirit
and the tolerance of all members. Everyone wanted to cable good
stories but on the whole the party-line, in the interest of the Game,
was maintained, and apart from a brief period, after the Referee
dispute, Manager Brooks was most co-operative.

It was cold at the famous De Beers Sports Ground for the game
v. Griqualand West. Although the sun shone, the wind blew
across the ground into the shadow of the stand and the press box.
Paul Irwin and myself sat next to the S.A.B.C., with cheerful
Chick Henderson in charge as Charles Fortune was away at the
Durban July, being a man of many parts, and wise enough to put
his money on William Penn who came second! We heard the
result before the start of the Griquas match and this did not
improve our demeanour, but it recalled for me the time in 1955
when we were given three horses for the Durban July, and they
came in one-two-three, and Vivian and myself forgot to put the
money on, which was very hard to take later in the day! This
match against Griquas was unspectacular, although won comfortably and after his good display against the Northern Transvaal,
I felt that Gibson and his midfield men did not 'flow' as they
should have done. Roux did perhaps tackle Gibson a shade late

with a low 'flyer' and slightly injured the Irishman's ankle, that temporarily revived memories of the 'Sharp Affair' which is still discussed hotly in South Africa. After the match the evening meal at the hotel was enlivened by the 'Wreckers' Club, who used Jack Horn's departure as the excuse for special dispensation.

Sunday July 7

We said goodbye to Kimberley but had to wait a while at the airport for the 727 from Johannesburg which had second replacement Bryan West aboard. While waiting, the 'Wreckers' turned to 'burners' and, with gas-jet cigarette-lighters, set fire to most of the Sunday papers being carried by fellow Lions, and when the plane was boarded, there was evidence of much 'burning'. On board, a section of the team had a cheese and wine party, before the usual warm welcome was received at Cape Town where the traditional happy faces of many friends and officials greeted the Lions in beautiful summer-like conditions. Sylvia and Vivian Duggan, ever faithful, were there and arranged for an afternoon drive around the peninsula, when work was done. The New Fairmead Hotel provided me with a comfortable, quiet room on the fourth floor and this was an encouragement to work hard during the next eight days.

The trip round the peninsula was magnificent and Bob Taylor joined us to explore the beauty of Hout Bay and the attraction of controversial Simon's Town. Is there a fairer cape in all the world? I'll say 'no' and anyway Sir Francis Drake was a far superior judge of beauty! Here I would claim that Cape Town is the most beautiful city in Southern Africa with a European population of 305,000 in its total of 807,200, but unlike other South African cities it has 417,000 coloured folk. It is a gentle place; a quiet place, without the hardness of many other big cities in the world. Its beauty compares with that of Vancouver, San Francisco, Naples, Rio and many others, and the backcloth of Table Mountain captures your heart from whatever angle you gaze at it. The road system, taking you in and out of the city, is an object lesson to modern planners, while shop keepers and hoteliers are there to please. The city is international and the blocked Suez Canal ensures a full harbour of ships for bunkering and victuals. The Cape has something extra, although one's thoughts often turned north to other beautiful things. Strange, but of the provincial unions, the Western Province was the most casual; independent, and but for good liaison officers like 'Porky' and 'Fairy' it would be a struggle, certainly for the touring press.

Monday July 8

Match day again; this time to Wellington to play Boland, and to the second most picturesque ground in the world, for I place the Commonwealth Stadium in Vancouver and Newlands as joint-firsts, especially if you are sitting in the Railway Stand at Newlands. At Vancouver the backcloth of the mighty Rockies is quite devastating but at Wellington the Drakenstein mountains are also good. The town is 44 miles from the Cape with a population of 10,000 and is the headquarters of the Boland provincial side which has always provided strong opposition for the Lions. The town is developing rapidly as an industrial centre with wine still the main product. Indeed, the adjacent town of Paarl is the centre of the South African wine industry and the home of Boy Louw and Gordon Bagnall, two excellent friends of many years. Boy Louw is a 'father confessor' of present South African rugby, beloved by all in the game, while Gordon Bagnall is an expert on many things, a brilliant scholar, and P.R.O. to the Nederburg Estate. He told Vivian and myself much about wine and how to judge and buy it, while we sat in the delightful old Dutch Farmhouse in the middle of the estate, with his wife Dorothy. Vivian had published in the *Cape Times* that we would have a picnic lunch at Wellington, but some other guests 'carried' the baskets off in error. We were hurriedly supplied with fresh ham sandwiches and beer by Jeff Reynolds, which were enjoyable, but not quite up to Mackeurtan standards at Pretoria, for that was better than Twickers! The match was won by the Lions but at considerable expense, for Gareth Edwards badly tore a hamstring in the closing minutes and this injury was to prove a decisive factor in the Third Test match defeat that was to follow. Perhaps he should not have been risked in this match as Gibson was being rested. Had Edwards not played we may have won the Third Test, and the playing of matches in the week of a test became the topic of discussion once again. Back at the New Fairmead Hotel in Rondebosch the 'Wreckers' were at it again; this time they were burning the shirts, of players and press, but Vivian and myself, as 'seniors', were given a free passage to our rooms!

PLATE 20. The two faces of Jeff Young. *Top:* Conducting the Bantu band during a visit to a gold mine on the Reef early in the tour

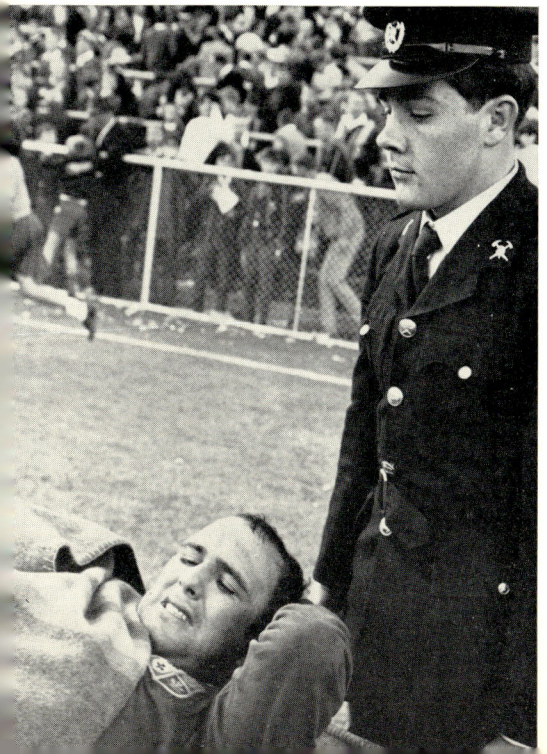

PLATE 21. *Below:* Being carried from the field on a stretcher after injuring his back towards the end of the First Test at Pretoria

PLATE 22. The Battle of Springs. *Left:* Referee Bert Woolley (centre) parts O'Shea and Brits, and orders O'Shea from the field in the second half of the match against Eastern Transvaal

PLATE 23. *Right:* After oranges and cushions had been thrown at O'Shea by a certain section of the crowd, Tony Horton (centre) and Ronnie Dawson move in to escort the player from the field

PLATE 24. *Left:* As soon as O'Shea reached the mouth of the tunnel leading to the dressing-room, he was struck by an irate spectator. Here he (No. 3) is struggling to get through the melée with the support of Dawson, Haydn Morgan, Rodger Arneil, and the police. McBride, first to his aid, is hidden by a policeman

Tuesday July 9

It was obvious today that Edwards was out of the Third Test and that Young would play at scrum half. The South African selectors brought back François Roux to the centre and dropped Dirksen, moving Nomis out to the wing. They did not drop Visagie at outside half and kept the same pack of forwards. For the Lions Telfer was still on the doubtful list following his knee trouble at Pretoria. The Lions had a stern practice and then visited the wine growing area at Stellenbosch. During the evening the Oxford and Cambridge graduates with the party were the guests of the local association and Gordon Bagnall welcomed them in amusing style. The weather was perfect and as one typed away merrily, the turtle doves' cooing notes echoed across the lovely area of Rondebosch. Life was pleasant and as the tension of pre-match test fever grew one sensed that it would be the 'big one' on the Saturday, and that the Lions were in with a chance. Tickets were scarce; incredibly so, and we just hoped that someone would come across some tickets somewhere as the Western Province Union were not as generous to players and press as the other three unions who staged tests. The British Press were able to purchase two tickets in the end while the Lions got two each and Springboks five each! The Lions were filling Newlands and putting thousands of pounds into the coffers of the local union. Obviously there is need for much re-thinking in the W.P. committee room. Jo'burg, Pretoria and Port Elizabeth can teach them a thing or two in this vital matter. Again, I hear that former Springboks, from outside Western Province, were not treated all that well. This is unfortunate at the 'cradle' of South African rugby.

Wednesday July 10

The Lions test team was announced and showed five changes from that which drew the Second test. Richards and Davies were in for Hinshelwood and Bresnihan; Stagg for Larter; Coulman for Millar to produce an all-England front-row for the first time in a test since the war; Young at scrum half for Edwards, and Telfer declared fit. It seemed a good side on paper, if it played to form, although the loss of Edwards was a blow, well though Young had survived at Pretoria against the Northern Transvaal. Coulman had deserved his first test call although Millar was not quite one hundred per cent fit. Much was expected of Davies in the centre, although it was a close call between Bresnihan and Turner. There were still several not lucky enough to win a test place, and Delme Thomas was disappointed, but did not expect what was to follow for him on the Saturday. After this selection only six players in the party, excluding West, had not won a test place at this stage of the tour, and the number was to be reduced to five when Thomas later appeared as a substitute for Coulman during the actual match. Max Baise was chosen as the referee and this proved a popular choice after his handling of the First Test. Goodall had surgery again on his injured hand to set his thumb properly and it was announced he would remain behind at Cape Town and leave for home from there when given full clearance at Groote Schuur Hospital. During the evening the Lions attended a 'Kalifa' at the Luxurama Theatre as the guests of the Montrose Sports Club and they had an enjoyable evening.

Thursday, July 11

The Test team had a training session in the morning and all went well. There were many spectators watching and during the afternoon the Springboks practised while the Lions travelled by cable car to the top of Table Mountain. There were a few patches of mist but all the party appeared to enjoy themselves for it is a fascinating experience. I had to make several important phone calls to Johannesburg but found the lines clear and fixed time calls prompt in answering.

Friday, July 12

This was the last chance for the Lions to brush up on their tactics and D–1 is always a nervous day for both sides. The Press gang make up their minds as to which side is going to win (I must admit now to fancying a draw), and cables depart to all parts of the world. The Lions were confident, and even the South African pressmen felt this was the test the Lions would win. There were no withdrawals although Engelbrecht was considered a gamble after injuring his ankle in training the previous day. The sun still shone as it had done all the week and I became very attached to my room. As I worked away I thought what a nice place the Cape was to work and live in. However, we were indeed lucky to enjoy such a run of good weather, which is normally most changeable there in July. During the evening we attended the South African Board's welcome party at Thibault House in the city and it was a most enjoyable affair with so many outstanding former players in attendance. Danie Craven welcomed the team, the press, and rugby V.I.P.'s from many parts, and Dewi Griffiths presented the BBC colour films of the first two Tests to the Board. On the way home Cliff, Vivian and myself called at the home of good friends in the game, Louis and Iris Babrow, to chat about previous visits to each other's countries, while Louis took several 'instant' colour shots which amused us.

Saturday, July 13

This was THE match day and the hotel was a noisy place. I phoned Gwen to wish her many happy returns, as it would be her birthday on the Monday and we would be travelling to East London. It was a clear line and a happy call, and Wayne was at home to discuss the match, briefly, and when he asked if the Lions would win, I replied, 'I feel they could draw!' Strange, but I was not entirely convinced that they could win, but surprised by the manner in which the match turned on the failure of the British backs. Vivian and myself lunched with friends at the magnificent Kelvingrove Club which is alongside Newlands, before taking our seats in glorious technicolour weather. What a remarkable contrast to Cardiff or Twickenham in January!

It was one of the saddest tests I have ever watched from a Lion's viewpoint, for they could and should have won. It was a chance in a lifetime, so well did the forwards play, but the four midfield backs did not rise to the occasion and this was especially true of Gibson. The task of preparing the cables afterwards even found me in a mood of depression, despite a long and bitter experience as a recorder of Lions defeats in many parts of the world. The cocktail party was so full that one could not get near to the doors, let alone get in to hear the speeches, but there could be no excuses from the Lions this time. Indeed, they offered none for they just threw the match away. Thus after a year of preparation the series was lost in 80 minutes, by a side that failed to rise to the occasion behind the scrum, apart from Kiernan and Savage. Even the substitution of lock Delme Thomas, for the injured prop Coulman, did not in any way weaken the forward effort. Cliff and myself walked back to the New Fairmead Hotel, and in twenty minutes pin-pointed the weaknesses. Test matches are lost on errors, but it takes great players to win them. The Lions had few behind the scrum, but worst of all, the two injured Welsh halves, John and Edwards, would in all probability have won the match. I retired to bed early, but heard the 'Wreckers' at work and their battle-cry, 'The wreckers are coming!' It was a sad day in British rugby history, July 13, and Herbert Waddell was most straightforward in his criticism. One does not always agree with Herbert's theories, but he was right this time. How sad for all those South Africans who really wanted the Lions to win this one. As I read in bed a tale about Jutland, to forget – if only for an hour – the sadness of defeat in the vital match, I wished I had been at home, sitting back with a 'quiet' whisky, watching TV. Perhaps, even such an experienced traveller as the 'Admiral', was homesick. It must have been the 6,000-mile telephone call in the morning!

Sunday, July 14

The Sunday papers told the story of the Lions defeat. There were many pictures and everyone asked, 'Who punched Pullin?' What a way to play rugby. It was a disgusting punch. Richards was kicked on the ground by another player, with the ball many yards away. Why do test players resort to such tactics? I can never understand this when they are not acts of retaliation. The morning and afternoon was spent working, sandwiching a pleasant lunch in the grill room as guest of Jeff Reynolds. For an hour Jimmy White, Jeff, Cliff, Vivian and myself discussed the match and then Cliff practised *It's a Wonderful World!* at the piano. At that moment it was not a wonderful world for the Lions, but Louis Armstrong always inspires enthusiasm. During late afternoon I travelled by car with Sylvia and Vivian Duggan to obtain different views of Table Mountain during a rather special sunset from Blaauwberg Bay. This certainly took my mind off the test. Then a chat with Group-Captain Cheshire about his work, and finally a quiet dinner at the Duggans' home.

Monday, July 15

We bid farewell to Jeff Reynolds, his wife Marjorie, Dick Hawkes and the staff and set off for the D.F. Malan Airport and a pleasant trip to East London, with a brief champagne party *en route!* Phillip and Shirley Jones, Dave Field and many other old friends met us at the airport, and these included one of the best rugby brains in South Africa and certainly one of their best captains, Basil Kenyon. I stayed with the Jones for a couple of nights and chatted about newspapers and the profession at home and in South Africa. The evening was spent visiting leading hotels, eating spots and night clubs, and there must be more in East London, per head of population, than in any other town in South Africa!

Tuesday, July 16

It was really warm today with the temperature in the 80's. It was summer to us who were visitors. There was an all-Welsh visit to a primary school by Cliff, Gareth Edwards, Keri Jones and myself. It was Selborne School where the two Jones boys and John Kenyon attended and we enjoyed it as much as the boys. I asked the boys to ask questions of the panel and if they were good questions they won a Lions badge! Then lunch at the King's Hotel and drinks in the open. Dewi and Cliff were brave enough to swim in the hotel's pool, but as it was in the shade, the water was really cold. During the evening we dined with the Kenyons and then watched the Springs match on the BBC Two film. An excellent evening. During a phone call to Johannesburg I was cut off after a certain time, as the switchboard operator said, 'You have had long enough!' I said to myself, 'It's a wonderful world!'

Wednesday, July 17

Another match day and another sad one. The best thing about it was the wonderful new Press box at the Border R.U. ground. This was almost as good as the new one at Lord's although, naturally, not as large, but it contained every amenity. It was regrettable that the match v. Border did not emulate the Press box accommodation in standards! The Lions played as if the reaction of the test defeat weighed upon them heavily. They won easily enough by 26 points to 6, but Robert 'Bossman' Hiller scored 23 of the 26 points with as good a display of kicking as I have ever seen from a Lion. It is true that the pressure was not on, as in a test, but he was the match-winner, looking the only class player behind the scrum, on either side. He kicked five penalties, converted the only try scored, and dropped two fine goals. However, the Lions lost Roger Young with two broken ribs after he was tackled into the crowd and fell across someone's knee, sitting within a yard of the touch line.

He carried on until half-time but then had to retire, and as soon as his injury had been confirmed after the match, Manager Brooks dashed up to the Press box and everyone had to re-write their stories! It was 'blood, sweat and tears' for another hour as the story of the third request for a replacement was sent off to the British Isles. It was to be Gordon Connell of Scotland, who had won his first cap in the previous March against England. As Brooks said, 'I've got to have someone!' Quietly, Edwards and John told me that they did not think they would be fit in time for the test, and so it looked like Connell, or a forward, in the specialist position at Ellis Park on July 27. When the work was over we had a meal, a pleasant one, at Deal's Hotel with the Kenyons and the Jones, and left as the Lions arrived. A comedian in the cabaret, Garth Meade, was excellent. The best South African I had heard, witty, modern, and extremely versatile. There were bangs in the nights as the 'Wreckers' went about their deadly business and many who were abed this night, worried that they would be 'visited'!

Thursday, July 18

Off to Bloemfontein in the 727 after a champagne party in the Carlton Hotel foyer. An innovation started by Jenkins and Thomas, long ago, but still an excellent way of saying *au revoir* and leaving one's hosts happy. Bloemfontein was warm and pleasant, and the large number of letters awaiting with news from home and abroad cheered one immensely. There was news, too, of another 'invasion' by the popular Mackeurtan Group which cheered and, as it rarely rains in Bloemfontein, there was every prospect of another picnic lunch! They said they would stay at the President Hotel; a new one which turned out to be the best in the Free State, apart from the Oppenheimer Cottage at Welkom! The end of the tour was very much in sight now, but as Connell left London today for South Africa, the management delayed the announcement of Saturday's team until the morrow.

Friday July 19

Everyone spent the day anxiously waiting for news of Gordon

Connell and eventually it was ascertained, that he had reached Johannesburg. Would he be played or held back? Coach Dawson said they would wait and speak to him, but later it was decided, wisely, to allow Connell to sleep first; rid himself of the effects of the long air flight, and leave the side to oppose Free State with an 'A. N. Other' at scrum-half. It was good to meet former Springbok Piet Wessels again, now news editor of the *Friend*, an excellent fellow, and to visit Signal Hill. Bloemfontein is a busy city with an interesting history, and centre of the vast Free State, but the people are kindly. During the evening the Fizzers gave the Group a party in return for previous hospitality, and as it is always difficult to return hospitality in South Africa, this was an achievement. Dewi gave a notable recital in the main hall of the President Hotel until the piano started disintegrating through no fault of his own, or indeed the 'wreckers'!

Saturday July 20

The match today was against Orange Free State, and after breakfast it was announced that Connell would play and receive his baptism less than 24 hours after touch-down and at a high altitude. This was a severe test but he appeared quite happy. The weather was warm and dry and the pitch hard and dusty, with the crowd of twenty-five thousand lost in the vast Free State arena. The picnic lunch outside was a great success and all the Group listened to the recorded programme of Cliff telling his life story to South African listeners. He pulled no punches and this was good, for listeners really learned what Welshmen are like: tenacious, independent, good talkers and occasionally, charmers! The match was a disappointment and as soon as it ended, Vivian received a message from London that the 'behaviour bubble' had burst on the front page of the *Sunday Times* in Johannesburg. He scampered off by car to interview Manager Brooks at the reception, while I was able to wait until later.

Brooks was taken by surprise but defended himself and his team, and Vivian sent off his message. The rest of the Press Gang awaited the arrival of the morning train with copies of the Jo'burg *Sunday Times*, spending the late evening at the only night club in Bloemfontein. Yet it was a pleasant one with good food and a smooth dance floor, and although some of the 'Wreckers' were there they did not succeed because of 'Lloyd's Law', now

universally enforced on rugby tours. However, it was a cold walk
back from one hotel to another in the early hours of the morning,
since the drop in temperature on the high veld in South Africa is
considerable.

Sunday July 21

After an early breakfast there was a rush to the news stall at
the Railway Station to obtain copies of the Jo'burg *Sunday
Times*. Even V.I.P.s on holidays were in the 'hunt' for the sensational news. When we got the paper, there it was, across the top
of the front page in a banner headline – 'Lions Behaviour Shocks
City' ... 'Hotel man tells of "unmitigated drunken revelry".' The
opening paragraph read, 'The touring Lions rugby party have left
a trail of havoc and stunned incredulity after three days in East
London marked by severe drinking bouts and riotous behaviour
at hotels and night clubs. They left broken hotel doors, broken
glasses by the dozen, unpaid liquor debts and girls in tears because
of outright rudeness.' After a life time of travel, and of meeting
people and players in all countries, I was amazed at this attack.
I personally had never read the like about any touring team in
any grade.

It was good to know, even before one read it, that a responsible
and experienced journalist like Paul Irwin, who was very much
a member of the Press Gang, had nothing to do with it.
The *Sunday Times* were in my view unwise to print it, and it
caused a great deal of trouble to all concerned. It was not a story
that the Press Gang enjoyed following up. At the hurried Press
Conference at the Maitland Hotel, Brooks said he would have to
investigate each allegation and then report later but that it was
all news to him. The Lions did crash in a door or two on tour
and break several glasses but what rugby team on tour, six
thousand miles away, has not 'kicked over the traces' occasionally?
This front page story almost made them appear to be international
criminals. It was a controversial form of journalism is a country
where rugby is a 'best-seller'. I am most ready to admit that such
stories on sport sometimes appear in the British Press, but I felt
the *Sunday Times* lost prestige in the eyes of many of its readers
after this sensational story.

The British Press Gang got their cables away hurriedly and
then travelled by charter plane, a Dakota, flown by a cheerful

Ulsterman, to Cradock in the North East Cape where a wonderful welcome awaited everyone on the air strip in the middle of a flat field. There were hundreds of cars and almost the entire population of the town. Why is it that so many of the smaller towns in the world are friendlier than the large cities. Is the struggle for existence in the cities too great, with little time to say 'how do' to your neighbours? The theme song of the tour was 'It's a wonderful world', and in Cradock the image was much nearer to this truth than in the larger cities. In the hotel everyone was friendly and the town was most attractive, but at night it was cold and the Press Gang had to resort to hot water bottles!

Monday July 22

Another match day *v.* North Eastern Districts – and in the week of the final test! All tours should leave the final week free, because playing and travelling within six days of a test is too much for any team in any country at the end of a tour.

During the morning I visited the station with the team's travel adviser, Jan Venter, and booked two night sleepers on the giant express from Port Elizabeth to Johannesburg which called at Cradock at 11.0 p.m. and was most suitable for Vivian and myself. Every tour in any country should include at least three train rides on the leading expresses, for too much air travel, however quick and efficient, does bore one and does not permit a good look at the countryside. A train journey provides an excellent opportunity, and every side visiting South Africa should travel at least once on the famous 'Blue Train' from the Cape to Johannesburg, or the reverse route. The comfort is considerable and the food magnificent.

The match against the North Eastern Cape, led by that admirable Springbok prop, Hannes Marais, proved an enjoyable one even though the Lions ran up their largest total of the tour. There was some good football from both sides and 'bossman' Hiller, to the delight of his colleagues and the Press Gang, notched his 100 points for the tour. It had taken him only eight matches; a splendid effort. There was an enjoyable reception afterwards at which Brooks hit out at the 'Sensational' Press. Immediately the 'Busy Beaver' of the tour, the likeable and sincere Sam Merwis was away to the telex room in another part of the stand, to send out the words of reply to all the criticisms. At least it cleared the air, and everybody was happier for something having been said. Local officials and friends were delighted. Before we took the night train to the city of Gold, we had an amusing game of snooker in the Cradock club, where Wales, represented by Vivian and myself, defeated South Africa, represented by Paul Irwin and Sam Merwis, but in all honesty I must record that it was Vivian and Paul who played the snooker, and a late rally by Vivian won the match! Then it was away to the train; a few brandies and dry ginger and the telling of tales and the recalling of our many trips together on trains. It was 2.30 a.m. before we retired for the night!

Tuesday July 23

We awoke at seven as the express raced, at 50 m.p.h., towards Bloemfontein and when we arrived there an hour later, the morning papers were provided. A half-an-hour stop and we were on our way. The breakfast at 55 cents (approximately 6s. 6d.) was excellent and the dining car staff most courteous. The countryside of the Free State which rolls along with plains and mealie fields punctuated by kopjes, was interesting to both of us, and the vastness of it all made us both wonder as to the future of the Republic. Then there was lunch at 65 cents, remarkable meal for the money, and back for a quiet nap before getting ready for Johannesburg. First, however, came a stop at Vereeniging where we had such a wonderful time in 1955, at the start of that brilliant tour, and then to the new station at Jo'burg. The trip had taken 17 hours, but was much enjoyed. We were met by the Group and then had an enjoyable social evening in the Northern Suburbs, where everyone is so glad to see visitors from the British Isles. The Jo'burg *Star* carried a story I had prepared under the heading, 'Give the Lions a Break,' in which I pointed out that all young men like to 'whoop it up' and that those of us who criticise should remember this. I asked the Ellis Park crowd to give them a big hand, for they deserved it. They had received enough punishment and criticism, far more than they merited.

Wednesday July 24

The test team was announced, with Delme Thomas included at tight head prop, and Horton as loose head. Otherwise the side was much as expected, for in many ways the team picked itself. I would have played Jarrett in the three-quarter line myself for he would have been fresh and eager, and Turner, Bresnihan and Gibson in midfield had not over-impressed in previous matches. The team trained hard and they appeared confident enough. However, the pressures were mounting as they started negotiations for presents to take back with them. The big shopping week was on. During the evening the Lions party and press were entertained by the British Consul at Hyde Park and among the guests were Gordon and Mary Waddell.

Thursday July 25

Johannesburg is the City of discount, for if you know the right people you can always purchase something below cost price. Naturally, this is always a great help to rugby visitors, and most of the Lions were well treated in this respect. Yet the shopping and packing, bidding farewell to friends from all over the Republic, took its toll. This appears to affect every touring team in the same way, with the players becoming tired as well as excited about the thought of returning home. Springbok coach Johan Claassens, not given to saying many words, told us that he was preparing plans to combat the Lions line-out specialists. This was a challenge the Lions expected. Coach Dawson said the Lions would make a special effort and were in with a chance. Actually at this stage the odds were against the Lions, much as they wanted to win. The Welsh group of supporters were hoping for a good match, as they were disappointed at what they had seen, as the rugby had lacked sparkle. Everyone hoped for an outstanding final test.

Friday July 26

The day before a big test is always a busy one, as the Press Gang prepare their previews, talk to management and players, and generally seek a way to find out what will happen on the morrow. The Lions headquarters must have answered hundreds of telephone calls and players were besieged by friends they had met on the way, seeking tickets. Many were busy writing thank-you letters and it really was a busy day. Manager Brooks took time off before lunch to entertain the travelling press and this was appreciated – there were many wise-cracks about 'broken glasses' etc! Everyone in the Lions party had an early night, waiting for the morrow.

There was just a chance the Lions would pull it off, but only a chance, as the backs would have to play really well.

Saturday July 27

This was the last match day and still the sun shone brightly. The hotel was seething with people from an early hour. Ian Todd, Cliff and myself went shopping, and as Gwen would say... 'We were all rushing round like blue a— flies, getting nowhere.' It was important shopping for presents for those near and dear. Then a quick and amusing picnic lunch with the Group and the Fizzers in Schweppes Yard, by kind permission of Ernie Franks, before we walked a few yards to Ellis Park, the scene of so many enjoyable matches for the Lions. The ground looked good and the organisation perfect, and when the teams fielded came the realisation that we really were on the last leg of the tour.

The match was enjoyable but the Springboks were far too good for the Lions on the day. The first half was even, but for ten minutes in the second half the Springboks dominated, took charge of the match, and finished worthy winners. The Lions forwards worked hard without winning too much ball, but the backs again disappointed and two more good scoring chances went abegging. The sending of the cables at the end of a series, without a victory to record, has become inevitable for me. Yet it is still a sad task. So many things were sad this day. One asked the question... 'Will British rugby ever get back to the standard of 1955?' Everyone praised the Springboks but Jim Telfer, a veteran of many a hard match against touring teams, whispered to me, 'Really, it is only a lack of basic skills'. How right he was, for there is nothing else really wrong. After a few quiet drinks at Little Farm, it was to bed with one final thought. If British Rugby is to recover overseas there must be dedicated coaching from now until the next tour. There is no easy road back to success, but the Lions have not won a major test overseas since 1959. We read that France had fared no better in New Zealand and were beaten by penalty goals, while the French management complained about the referees there and law interpretations. Why does it always happen in New Zealand? Bertie Strasheim did a good job in the test, but then he is an excellent, experienced referee. There is still need of neutral referees in the Southern Hemisphere countries. Such a system must come eventually into being.

Sunday July 28

The morning was spent in preparing cables while the players packed. Cliff Dewi and their camera men did the last TV interviews. A final lunch in the Northern Suburbs for the Fizzers – this time at Murrae and John Cowley's – was much enjoyed, and then in the late afternoon the 'cortege' moved off to the Jan Smuts Airport, where thousands of cheerful South Africans, including the Group, bade farewell to the Lions as they marched out to their VC.10. It was a comparatively happy send-off, for the Lions were convinced that they were not as bad as the Johannesburg *Sunday Times* made them out to be. Indeed they were not, but neither were they a great side. They were often a good side, and a brave one, but they lacked so much behind. Injuries prevented them from being better than they were. It is often so with British touring teams. Up into the moonlight night they went, singing and talking, and I suppose, reflecting upon their eleven weeks tour. The last page of the Diary closed. It was all a little sad.

PART THREE

The Twenty Matches
(Comment, scorers and teams)

PLATE 25. Robert Barnard, the Transvaal hooker, touches down for the try that sealed the fate of the tourists in their only provincial defeat

PLATE 26. Lions v. Northern Transvaal. The vital try, which gave the Lions new hope, being scored by prop forward Mike Coulman early in the second half. Coulman, lying flat over the goal-line, has just peeled off and charged over from a line-out

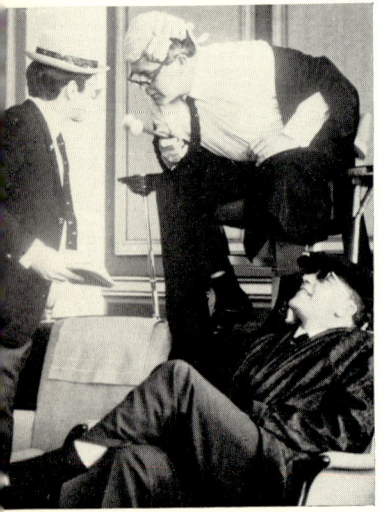

PLATE 27. *Top left:* All dressed up for the official team photograph at Sea Point, Cape Town. Sandy Hinshelwood 'models' the regulation Lions' playing attire. PLATE 28. *Top right:* Brave Roger Young enters the Indian Ocean in mid-winter! Actually the water is warmer than on the Cornish beaches in mid-summer. PLATE 29. *Left:* Mr 'Justice' O'Shea holds court on a Sunday morning somewhere in Southern Africa. He appears to be discussing a difficult technical point with his legal aid, Gerald Davies, while court treasurer, Sid Millar, awaits developments! PLATE 30. *Below:* Into battle. The 'old' travellers, Vivian Jenkins and the Author, ready for the First Test at Pretoria, wearing mining headgear, suitably inscribed

The Twenty Matches

(Comment, scorers and teams)

First Match
Versus Western Transvaal at Olen Park, Potchefstroom,
Saturday May 18.
Lions won by a goal, two penalties and three tries (20) to four
penalties (12).
Weather: Fine and sunny. *Ground:* Firm. *Crowd:* 20,000.
Teams:
WESTERN TRANSVAAL: B. Blignaut; I. Schutte, G. Vogel, G.
Pearson, C. van der Merwe; P. due Randt, J. de Jager; J.
Voljoen, R. McKechnie, B. Lowe, T. G. Kruger, J. Nel,
E. Claassen (capt.), A. Bates, M. Wilkens.
BRITISH ISLES: T. J. Kiernan (capt.); W. K. Jones, J. W. C.
Turner, T. G. R. Davies, M. Richards; C. M. H. Gibson,
G. Edwards; M. J. Coulman, J. Young, A. L. Horton, R. B.
Taylor, W. D. Thomas, W. J. McBride, M. G. Doyle,
J. W. Telfer.
Referee: A. P. Bird (Western Transvaal).

After a week of rain, conditions were perfect for the match –
the last of six fixtures to be played on Olen Park that day. A
crowd of 20,000 packed the ground to capacity and there was a
five minute delay before the kick-off and one wondered whether
a change had had to be made in the Lions side. However, they
fielded as selected and the Western Transvaal kicked off to start
the tour. An exciting moment and an important one, especially
for Messrs Brooks and Dawson who had worked so hard for
twelve months in preparing for this great moment.

The first scrum was won by the Lions on the tight-head and it
was the first of a dozen by the Horton-Young combination, but
after seven minutes the Westerns were in the lead. Following a
scrum infringement 30 yards out, outside-half du Randt kicked a
good penalty goal, but Kiernan kicked wide with his first attempt.

Du Randt kicked wide with another attempt and then, after 25 minutes, Blignaut landed a penalty goal after Taylor had fallen off-side at a wheeled scrum.

Just before the interval the Lions got their first points of the tour and it was fitting that these should be scored by the genial Jim Telfer. Gibson found a beautiful touch, down in the left-corner, where the Lions won the ball off the Westerns' throw-in, and Telfer peeled-off to the front of the line smartly, to dive over in the corner for the first try. Kiernan failed with the conversion and also with another penalty attempt when Gibson was obstructed yet again. The Westerns moved during the kick and it was re-taken, but poor Kiernan missed yet again which brought his tally of misses to five!

The Westerns led by two penalties to a try at the interval but there was no cause for alarm at this stage. The Lions forwards had improved slowly during the first-half and won several tight head strikes as Horton and Young combined smartly. Gibson had played within himself and appeared to be holding something back for the second-half. Had Kiernan kicked some of his goals the Lions would have been well in the lead.

The popular captain made amends early in the second-half when with his sixth attempt he landed a fine penalty goal from 45 yards and a wide angle. The Lions were square now and soon went ahead. Edwards picked up smartly after a loose heel and sent Gibson away, running to the wide blind side. Turner went with him and crashed over with the final pass but the kick failed.

The lead was short-lived for Randt kicked an easy penalty goal from a rather puzzling penalty award, but the Lions had a similar chance and this time, Gibson failed with the kick. After 15 minutes of the second-half Edwards went away swiftly from a ten yard scrum, again to the wide blind side and passed outside for the ball to bounce off a defender over the line. The zealous Telfer was up to get the touch down and this time Kiernan kicked the goal. He followed this with a 40 yard penalty and everyone was happy, but the Westerns hit back with another penalty through Randt, this time from 50 yards, and they were still in the match.

Before the Westerns scored this fourth and last penalty Gibson was carried off and he appeared to be in great pain. It looked as if he had broken his ankle, an accident that would have put him out for the tour, in a perfectly fair tackle. There was a pause of five minutes before Bresnihan appeared as the first official subsitute in international rugby, as allowed under the new law. There was a delay of nine minutes from the moment of injury to the arrival of the replacement, who had to dash down to the dressing-room and change, and everyone suggested later that four official substitutes on each side, should be changed in the stand, waiting in tracks suits so as to appear on the field immediately, if required.

The seven Lions forwards did their stuff and before the close another try was scored to make victory certain. Doyle got over but was recalled and then Edwards went away smartly from a wheeled scrum, drew defenders on to him, and fed the strong-running Turner who put the speedy Davies over for a good try, which was not converted. The final whistle soon sounded and the Lions had got away to a good start.

It was certainly better than at Invercargill in 1966, but there were weaknesses and David Brooks came straight to the press box to say, 'It was a good start but there is plenty to work on!' His was a realistic attitude but there were worries about the injury to Gibson and the effects of a hard tackle on Turner. The Lions had done better than anticipated; they had succeeded where the 1955 Lions had just failed, but at the cost of two players out for several matches. However, injuries have to be expected on a long tour at the rate of roughly two players a match and that is why thirty players are always taken on tour.

It was the overall speed of the side to the scene of the breakdown that impressed South African critics, plus their ability to strike quickly in the set scrums and run elusively behind.

Second Match
Versus Western Province at Newlands, Cape Town, Wednesday May 22.
Lions won by two goals (10) to a penalty and a try (6).
Weather: Sunny and warm. *Ground:* Firm. *Crowd:* 40,000.
Teams:
WESTERN PROVINCE: H. O. de Villiers; G. Brynard, E. Olivier, J. van der Merwe, J. Engelbrecht; H. Fabricius, H. van der Merwe; B. Neethling, C. Cockrell, A. Janson, J. Coetzee, J. Naude (capt.), D. van der Berg, G. Van Wyk, A. Thom.
BRITISH ISLES: T. J. Kiernan (capt.); M. Richards, T. G. R. Davies, F. P. K. Bresnihan, K. F. Savage; B. John, R. M.

Young; S. Millar, J. V. Pullin, A. L. Horton, R. Arneil,
P. K. Stagg, W. J. McBride, J. Taylor, J. W. Telfer.
Referee: M. Baise (Cape Town).

The match was played on the hottest autumn day I can recall
on several visits to Newlands. In fact it was the equal of a really
hot summer's day in the British Isles, and even though the kick-off
was at 4.0 p.m. it was extremely warm when the teams fielded. In
the days before the match Western Province officials were be-
moaning the fact that they had been allocated a mid-week fixture
against the Lions and not a Saturday date, and felt they would
not achieve the crowd or gate receipts of previous engagements.
The S.A. Board had adopted a new procedure for the tour, allow-
ing several smaller centres to have Saturday matches and the
larger ones to have provincial matches during mid-week.

However, the Western Province were blessed with good fortune
for on this Wednesday the fine weather and the lure of the
Lions brought spectators flocking to the turnstiles and at the kick-
off 40,000 were present, the second best gate at the ground during
mid-week, surpassed only by the Combined Universities *v.* Lions
classic of 1955 which attracted 43,000. Cheers greeted the
appearance of both sides and as the teams lined up one felt the
tour was really on, and that the Lions were in action at last.

There had been an exciting curtain raiser between the Cape
Town and Stellenbosch Universities 'under twenty' teams and
there was quite a number of good players on view including a
powerful Stellenbosch wing, Muller, and Neil, the son of Louis
Babrow, former Springbok and coach to the Western Province
side. Danie Craven was present and he saw Stellenbosch lose,
which was sad for him but both Danie Craven and Louis Babrow
must have been sorry to see Western Province lose.

The Lions won and deserved to do so, although many Cape
Town critics thought they were lucky. They may have been
fortunate in the closing stages, but overall they were the better
side. Western Province began magnificently but once their initial
attacks had failed they never attacked with quite the same gusto
although they got one good try in the second-half.

The Lions were handicapped for both Jim Telfer and John
Taylor were injured in the first-half, with leg injuries, but they
were patched up and struggled gamely until the close, because

the local doctor would not allow substitutes. In the second-half Gerald Davies was off with an injured achilles tendon but returned before the close and in all nine minutes of injury time was correctly played.

The Lions forwards were giving away some weight and shove for most of the match but won the tight head count 2–1 and in the end held an advantage at the line-out where Stagg, the Lions 'secret weapon', was successful. However there was too much tapping back from the line-out which caused Young at scrum-half much embarrassment but he coped adequately. Arneil had an excellent first match in a Lions' jersey while Millar and McBride, the 'old Irish firm', did well and Telfer and Taylor deserved a special mention for holding on so well in painful circumstances.

Barry John had an excellent match at outside-half. He made a try by moving away from a tight head-scrum on his own line; covered smartly and kicked shrewdly when the Lions were on the defensive. Perhaps he could have let the ball go more frequently as he just failed with three attempts at dropped goal, but I feel in this match, his first outside Europe and in the Lions jersey, he played to win, and as his side won and he played an important part, he was deserving of praise.

Indeed there were no failures in the Lions side, for the centres tackled really hard and Davies showed his flash of speed; the wings were always trying and got a try apiece, while Kiernan was safe and venturesome in turn at full-back although pressing too hard with his place kicking and failing with five penalty attempts.

The Western Province disappointed, for their forwards did not win much good quick possession until near the close and the traditional play at half-back which has made the Western Province one of the great sides in history was not in evidence. Van der Merwe at scrum-half was harassed and Fabricius at fly-half subdued, as if disappointed with his failure to kick two goals when the ball rebounded from the near upright on each occasion.

He did not read the game well, and kicked when he should have passed and *vice versa*, especially in the closing stages when the Lions tired a little and the Province won more possesion. It was then that the side needed inspired leadership with a touch of Craven or Osler, but Naude had run himself almost to a standstill by this time and the Province missed a few excellent chances.

Naude was the best Western Province forward and player, and he carried on throughout the second-half with a badly-cut head, looking like a wounded Indian chief. De Villiers at full-back revealed his lack of judgment and experience although he had been the idol of Newlands in 1967, while Engelbrecht, moving towards the end of a long and exciting career, found himself well-marked by Richards, an important factor in the match.

The refereeing of Max Baise, a panel member, was quite sound, although he tended to be a little theatrical at times with his indication of infringements. The Lions had no complaints on this score, and there was only one incident when prop Neethling wrestled with Richards long after the whistle had gone, but it is possible that he did not hear it blow, although the Referee spoke to him afterwards.

The Lions took the lead after twenty minutes with a good try started by an 'up and under' from John that worried de Villiers. There was a scrum and Taylor robbed Fabricius and dribbled away. Stagg was up to gather and send the ball out left to Bresnihan for Davies to carry on and put Richards over unopposed for a try that Kiernan converted, after failing with three penalty attempts in nine minutes.

After 34 minutes Tiny Naude almost kicked a lovely penalty goal from the half-way line to indicate the threat for the Lions if they infringed in their own half. Two minutes later the Lions scored again and this time Kiernan was not given a fair catch outside his own line. A scrum was ordered and the Lions won the tight-head for John to race away, kick-on, re-gather and kick on again. Van der Merwe tried to gather but was rushed by John and Richards. Then Richards gathered and fed Bresnihan on his right, who put Savage over under the posts for a try after a movement of 110 yards. Kiernan kicked the goal but Naude kicked a 50-yard penalty just before the interval and the Lions crossed over 10–3 in the lead.

There was one score in the second half, and then after 35 minutes, as the Lions tired. The Province won the ball at a maul and moving left, de Villiers entered the line to make the man over. Kiernan tackled him but centre Van der Merwe was up with the full-back and crossed for a good try. Fabricius saw his conversion attempt hit an upright and rebound back.

Try as they did the Province could not score the five points for victory and the Lions gained an important triumph. Two wins in the first two matches was an excellent start.

Third Match
Versus South-Western Districts at Mossell Bay, Saturday May 25.
Lions won by three goals, two penalties and a try (24) to two penalties (6).
Weather: Fine and sunny. *Ground:* Firm. *Crowd:* 10,000.
Teams:
SOUTH-WESTERN DISTRICTS: P. Kromhout; C. Uys, A. Stander, T. Stander, C. P. Pretorious; B. Puren, A. Horne; R. Derecksen (capt.), G. Olivier, J. Verster, J. Jamneck, M. Vlok, J. Vermeulen, D. Botha, D. Jonker.
BRITISH ISLES: R. B. Hiller; A. J. W. Hinshelwood, F. P, K. Bresnihan, W. H. Raybould, W. K. Jones; B. John, R. M. Young; S. Millar (capt.), J. Young, M. J. Coulman, R. Arneil, P. J. Larter, W. D. Thomas, M. G. Doyle, R. B. Taylor.
Referee: Dr W. C. Malan (Vredenburg).

The day of the match was more like the kind of day we get on an August Bank holiday in the British Isles, once in ten years, when everyone rushes down to the sea and there are ten mile traffic jams on the way home. The town of Mossell Bay was crowded and the road to the top of the hill, where the ground was situated, at its busiest. Cars were parked everywhere as people had left them hurriedly in order to gain a good position. As some spectators were there at 8 a.m. when the gates opened, the ground was full long before the Lions match, timed to start at 4 p.m. It presented a picturesque scene, much as if one was watching cricket at St Helen's at Swansea. The Indian Ocean simmered three hundred yards from the far touch-line and the historical Bay stretched away beautifully to the left although partly obscured by the heat haze.

The Lions did not intend taking the match easily although they expected to win it, for they knew the District forwards would not be easily tamed. The latter played hard and sternly under the leadership of Derecksen, but cleanly, and there was only one little flurry of blows over the touch-line. The Lions had to work hard for possession and when they did run they were well-marked and covered by the District men. Among these, no one tackled harder than Kromhout at full-back, Stander in the centre, Horne at scrum-half and Jonker at Number eight.

However in this match the Lions took the lead and held it throughout, and although leading by no more than 9–3 at the interval, ran out comfortable winners by 24–6 and the margin could have been larger. Millar kept the side well together and got them to move the ball readily once the District pack had been controlled, especially in the loose. It was the overall pace of the Lions that impressed once again and was the real reason for their victory. They used this to get to the ball quickly and feed the backs who were always in position.

It was a good début for Hiller who succeeded with five attempts out of nine, landing three conversions, almost from the touch-line, and two penalty goals. The ball was kicked easily and accurately and one attempt struck the top of the near upright. At full-back he was quite sound although more eager to join the backs in attack, than protect the 'box', towards the end of the match. As we watched him the thought occurred that he would press Kiernan hard for the Test position, unless the 'master' recaptured the kicking form that made him the toast of Australia.

Hinshelwood did well during his first match in South Africa and scored two tries while Raybould ran well but appeared a shade nervous, as he admitted afterwards, and this affected his handling a little. Bresnihan again impressed with his strong running and additional pace, and revealed he was bidding hard for a Test place. John made several spectacular lone runs in the first-half and then linked effectively with his threequarters in the second, but was again just wide with a drop at goal.

Of the forwards, Millar and Coulman were sound, energetic props; Larter and Thomas jumped well, and the back-row searched for the ball, with Arneil confirming the good impression gained at Newlands. They kept pace well in the heat, suggesting that the Dawson training schedule was achieving its objective. Referee Malan was a new official, having his first representative match in his first year on the panel. He was strict, but not at this time an international referee, for many matches are needed to get the feel of things. However he did not attempt to 'please' the Lions and was unbiassed.

Hiller kicked a 20 yard penalty goal after six minutes when the Districts put in to a scrum 'not straight', but Kromhout

PLATE 31. *Above:* The official travelling Press, TV and Radio party with the 1968 Lions, photographed at Cape Town (it needed a minor 'miracle' to get them all together). *Back row* (l. to r.): Ian Todd (*Sun*), David Frost (*The Guardian*), Phil Saayman (*Die Beeld*), Gerhard Viviers (*SAUK*). *Second row:* Charles Fortune (*S.A.B.C.*), John Reason (*Daily Telegraph*), Terry O'Connor (*Daily Mail*), John du Toit (*Transvaler*), Quintus van Rooyen (*Oosterlig*). *Sitting:* Paul Irwin (*Rand Daily Mail*), Vivian Jenkins (*Sunday Times* and *The Times*), Pat Marshall (*Daily Express*), Gert Kotze (*Die Vaderland*), Bryn Thomas (*Western Mail* and *Thomson Newspapers*), Ace Parker (*Argus Group*). *In front:* Dewi Griffiths (*BBC TV*), Sam Merwis (*S.A.P.A.*), Gert le Roux (*Dagbreek*), Cliff Morgan (*BBC TV* and *News of the World*). PLATE 32. *Below:* Mike Gibson and the team mascot outside Meikles Hotel, Salisbury, during the happy visit to the 'rebel' land!

PLATE 33. *Above:* The 'mini line-out' in operation. Peter Stagg beats Frik du Preez for the ball at a mini line-out of three forwards a side at Pretoria in the First Test. PLATE 34. *Below, left:* Gerald Davies, the Welsh centre, streaks away for the most brilliant try of the tour after running through the Boland team at Wellington. PLATE 35. *Below, right:* Thys Lourens, the Springbok flank forward, scores the vital try in the Third Test, which decided the series, at Cape Town. Following a tap back, Young was covered and Lourens gathered the loose ball to dive over despite the attentions of Gibson and Kiernan

equalised four minutes later amid loud cheers with an excellent goal from near the touch-line and forty yards out. After 19 minutes Hiller kicked a straight 27 yard penalty and six minutes later the Lions got their first try. John went away left for Bresnihan to change direction right, and get to the corner where he was tackled. Hinshelwood, in close support, gathered to dive over. Hiller hit the top of the upright with his conversion attempt.

Early in the second-half the Lions scored the important try quickly to move into a comfortable lead. John kicked high to his left. Doyle and Arneil were there to tackle the coverers, and Arneil put Jones over in the corner. This time Hiller kicked a fine conversion from the touch-line. Kromhout pegged back three points with another penalty goal from 35 yards after a line-out infringement before the Lions scored again. Hiller entered the line and Hinshelwood ran strongly before he was tackled for the ball to go loose, and Taylor gathered and raced over in the corner for Hiller to kick another fine goal from near the touch-line.

Before the end the Lions got their fourth try. This was started by Taylor, stepping back at Number eight, picking up, and feeding Young, who had a splendid match, moving swiftly down the blind side. Raybould joined in and put Hinshelwood over in the right corner. Hiller obliged with another good conversion and the Lions 15 points tally in the second half, had been worthily gained. They left the field contented for, as Millar said, 'We put the record right after our poor display at Oudtshoorn in 1962'.

Fourth Match
Versus Eastern Province at Boete Erazmus, Port Elizabeth, Wednesday May 29
Lions won by one goal, two dropped goals, three penalties and one try (23) to one goal, three penalties (14).
Weather: Fine, overcast. *Ground:* Firm. *Crowd:* 20,000.
Teams:
EASTERN PROVINCE: T. Adlan; M. Cowley, G. Norje, G. van Tander, G. C. Cilliers; A. Vosloo, S. Terblanche; R. Parker, S. Cloete, R. Smith, J. Hurter, G. Carelse (capt.), J. Rushmere, J. Dormehl, J. Englelbrecht.
BRITISH ISLES: R. B. Hiller; W. K. Jones, K. S. Jarrett, W. H. Raybould, A. J. W. Hinshelwood; J. W. C. Turner, R. M. Young; J. P. O'Shea, J. V. Pullin, M. J. Coulman, R. B. Taylor

E

(capt.), P. K. Stagg, P. J. Larter, M. G. Doyle, W. J. McBride.
Referee: C. de Bruyn (Transvaal).

The giant Boete Erazmus Stadium was one-third full when the
teams fielded below overcast skies after a bright morning and the
match was to prove exciting if not outstanding in quality. It contained many sparkling moments but also a great deal of scrappy
play and it was possibly a match that the Lions might have lost
without any real complaint. They deserved to win it in the end,
and their late rally left no doubt in the minds of watchers that
they would not be easily beaten.

The man of the match, who strangely enough could have lost it
but actually won it, was England full-back Bob Hiller who gave a
display, mixing brilliance and casualness, that was exciting and
entertaining. He kicked three penalties and one conversion, most
of them beautiful kicks from narrow angles, and also scored a try
by finishing off a movement he started outside his own line. His
approach to rugby is a gay one, with a true touch of the Barbarian
ideal, but in this match his attacking position in the threequarter
line, caused the heart to beat faster when the opposition kicked
over the back line to find the big wide open spaces where Hiller
should have been!

Yet one had to admire this gay young man, for his accurate
goal-kicking with the pressure on late in the match, was admirable
and an excellent example of a sound technique. In mid-field the
Lions were not too happy, for they lacked rhythm and drive. The
three midfield backs, Turner (playing at outside half), Raybould
and Jarrett, rather overdid the kick ahead in attack, and over-
elaborated in their passing movements.

The two fast-running wings, Jones and Hinshelwood, were not
given quick possession with room to move because the ball did not
flow along the line in 'chain passing'. It was Jarrett's first match
and he did not shape as well as he should have done, while
Raybould, normally a fine runner in broken play, appeared tenta-
tive.

We did not know at the time that Roger Young was suffering
from a groin injury even before play started, but had gamely
agreed to play because Edward's hamstring injury was still not
completely right. To make matters worse Young aggravated the
injury in the second-half while making a fine save in defence, but

he carried on, although it meant him missing several matches. Lions players from Ulster have a high reputation and there is no happier or more willing tourist than this good-looking dental student.

Bob Taylor suffered a kick above the knee, not in anger, and his speed about the field was reduced as he led a Lions side for the first time. Worse feature of the Lions forward play, which led them into a great deal of trouble, was their tapping back in the front and centre of the line-out. The Eastern Province forwards and especially hooker, Cloete, were quickly through the line to hamper Young, but at the end of the line McBride, playing as No. 8 quite effectively, and the continually improving Arneil, did well.

The scoring provides the story of the match, for Hiller kicked the Lions into the lead in the first minute of play when Eastern Province were penalised at the first maul from the kick off, with a 30 yard goal. Ten minutes later Turner dropped a high goal from 30 yards before the Eastern Province kicked their first penalty through full-back Adlam from 35 yards.

After 23 minutes the Lions scored a splendid try. Hiller started the movement from full-back and handed on to Jones, coming inside, for the wing to race through, survive a half tackle, and eventually hand on to Pullin. Jones took another pass from the hooker and then sent Hiller galloping 20 yards up the left touchline to score the try. Hiller did not convert this but the Eastern Province captain, giant second-row lock Carelse, landed a low 46 yard goal to reduce the Lions lead before the interval.

In the second-half the Lions started unhappily and allowed themselves to be harassed by the lively opposing forwards. After ten minutes Eastern Province were level through a 35 yard straight penalty goal by Carelse, after Young had been penalised at a scrum. Fortunately Hiller regained the lead two minutes later with a good 30 yard penalty and this was improved upon by another high dropped goal from Turner from 35 yards.

One expected the Lions to roar away now to a convincing win but after 27 minutes Eastern Province got to within a point of the Tourists. They had been pressing for some time and then went right from a loose maul to outflank the Lions defence, mainly because Hiller was out of position, and Van Tander put Norje over for a good try which Carelse converted.

The decisive score was made by McBride running from the back of a scrum to the open side and feeding Hinshelwood who just got over in the right corner. Hiller kicked a beautiful conversion from the touch-line and, before the close, kicked a third penalty after Stagg had been barged at a line-out. The Lions were home and dry but not before they had experienced many an alarm!

Fifth Match
Versus Natal at King's Stadium, Durban, Saturday June 1.
Lions won by one goal, one penalty, three tries (17) to one goal (5).
Weather: Warm, overcast. *Ground:* Firm. *Crowd:* 35,000.
Teams:
NATAL: R. L. Gould; N. Gibson, J. G. Bennett, M. R. Swanby, J. A. Koorts; R. Seymour, G. Giles; P. R. Ripley-Evans (capt.), D. C. Walton, W. A. Labuschange, T. P. Bedford, J. A. A. Kapp, M. C. J. van Rensburg, J. D. McIntosh, I. F. Grant.
BRITISH ISLES: T. J. Kiernan (capt.); M. C. R. Richards, J. W. C. Turner, F. P. K. Bresnihan, K. F. Savage; B. John, G. O. Edwards; S. Millar, J. V. Pullin, A. L. Horton, M. G. Doyle, P. K. Stagg, W. D. Thomas, R. Arneil, W. J. McBride.
Referee: Mr W. T. F. Lane (Natal).

This match proved to be a tale of two halves with the Lions brilliant in the first half and only fair in the second. They won convincingly enough and were never in danger of defeat but they lost their rhythm in the second half and towards the end had to defend desperately against spirited recovery by Natal. The Province has become famous for its grand-stand finishes, but in this match, though full of fire and energy, did not possess quite enough pace to outwit the Lions.

Barry John established himself as the number one outside half with a fine, well-controlled display of running rugby, that was to be short lived, as he was struck down by injury in the First Test, his fourth match of the tour. He set the Lions alight in the first half and there were some lovely tries scored which enabled the Lions to lead at the interval 17–0.

The ball flowed freely from forwards to halves and Edwards and John were in splendid form as a club and national pair, suggesting they would worry the Springboks if they enjoyed ready possession. Swift halves like these need good ball to set any match alight and the Lions forwards did remarkably well with Thomas, Horton, Arneil and McBride looking test players.

There were signs in this match that the Lions were developing into a more than useful side but it is only fair to record that Natal, without three of their leading backs, were not as strong as in past years, though still blessed with the same spirit of attack, and coached by the illustrious Izak van Heerden. Of all provincial sides in South Africa, the 'banana boys' of Natal, are the best at open football, and have been since the combination of van Heerden, Irvine and Oxlee. Had they been at full strength, and Oxlee still playing at his best, we would have had a better chance of judging the real strength of the Lions at this stage of the tour.

In the second half the Lions appeared to ease back the throttle and take things more easily which allowed Natal to recover. Perhaps there were signs here that should have warned us for the First Test, while Horton and Thomas were not to be included in the First Test team. Yet enough confidence was generated by the play of Edwards and John, and the swift breaks of Edwards against Springbok loose forwards like Bedford and Grant encouraged us all to believe that they could be a match-winning pair. Kiernan spent a great deal of the second-half potting at penalty goal in an effort to regain his accuracy, but each time he was just wide.

Richards and Savage on the wings were sharp and eager while Bresnihan, recently recovered from stomach trouble, and Turner were sound centres. Stagg won a lot of ball at the line-out and moved about in the loose, to suggest that he would develop into a real Test forward while McBride had a good day at No. 8. However the final rally by Natal was a pointer to certain shortcomings in the Lions side. Gould was extremely sound at full-back for Natal, despite his being one-footed, and his display won him a final Springbok trial and, eventually, a full cap. Actually the rally by Natal won trial places for half a dozen of their players and the eventual recall of the Springbok No. 8 and former Oxford captain, T. P. Bedford, who was honoured with the leadership of the Springbok pack.

The Lions took the lead after five minutes play when Edwards made a flashing break on the open side of a twenty yard scrum with an elusive diving run, to end up between the posts for a cracking try. Kiernan kicked an easy goal and five minutes later landed a 25 yard penalty. It was not long before John went away wide from a line-out and moving right sent an overhead pass to Savage who handed on to Turner running outside him and the Scot was over in the corner for a fine try.

Five minutes later, after Natal had failed with their third penalty attempt down wind, the Lions scored again. McBride went away in the loose, running powerfully and he handed on to Millar who sent Bresnihan dashing over for a good try. Kiernan could not convert this one nor the previous one by Turner, and it was just before the interval when the Lions scored their fourth try.

It was Edwards who went away again, running to the open side to draw the defence and hand on to Turner. He made ground and sent an overhead pass for Richards to race over in the corner. Again Kiernan kicked wide, as did Swanby with his fourth attempt at a penalty goal during the first-half. At the interval it was 17–0 to the Lions and changing round to have the wind behind them, we expected big things. On reflection it was sad that they did not add to their total and boost their own morale.

Edwards crossed early in the second-half but was recalled for a slightly forward pass before Kiernan just failed with three penalty attempts, which did not please the crowd, eager for open, running play. Ten minutes from the end Natal scored the try they deserved. They won a tight head scrum and moved sharply to the blind side, their wing Gibson sending the ball back inside to the supporting McIntosh, who crossed for a good try. This time Swanby kicked the goal and the Stadium rocked with applause. Soon they attacked again and Koorts dropped a pass on the right wing with the line at his mercy. It was exciting stuff and a bright end to a match that had started well and promised so much in the second-half without quite succeeding, but the Lions were still unbeaten.

Sixth Match
Versus Rhodesia at the Police Ground, Salisbury, Monday June 3.
Lions won by four goals, two penalties, one dropped goal, one try (32) to one penalty, one try (6).
Weather: Fine, breezy. *Ground:* Firm. *Crowd:* 18,000.
Teams:
RHODESIA: W. Herman; D. Smith, J. G. Jones, L. N. Denyer,

A. L. French; M. J. Martin, E. N. Alexander; R. H. Cloleshaw, R. G. Mundell (capt.), G. von Horsten, B. Murphy, R. Robertson, I. D. Fuller, R. J. Varkevisser, E. Hartley.
BRITISH ISLES: T. J. Kiernan (capt.); W. K. Jones, K. S. Jarrett, T. G. R. Davies, A. J. W. Hinshelwood; C. M. H. Gibson, G. O. Edwards; M. J. Coulman, J. Young, J. P. O'Shea, M. G. Doyle, W. D. Thomas, P. J. Larter, R. J. Arneil, R. B. Taylor.
Referee: Mr G. Robertse (Transvaal)

Of all the welcomes given on this tour to the Lions, on arrival at a ground, this was the best. Half an hour before the start the Lions walked along the touch-line *en route* to the dressing-room and, although it was during an interesting schools match curtain raiser, the whole crowd stood, including Prime Minister Ian Smith and his wife, and applauded and cheered. This was a spontaneous act of appreciation for the Lions determination in visiting the 'rebel' land and maintaining the true freemasonry and friendship of rugby football. As Cliff Morgan and myself stood up with the camera crew, high up on the TV platform, we were deeply touched by the show of emotion and the Lions told us afterwards that they, too, were deeply moved by the reception.

It must have disturbed their concentration for they took a long time to settle down against a lively, bustling Rhodesian side. In the second-half they recovered their poise but not before an hour's play had elapsed after leading at the interval by no more than six points to three. It was a tribute to the tenacity of the Rhodesians and especially their two halves, Alexander and Martin, who supported their forwards splendidly, while the back row covered and harassed effectively.

During the first-half, Gibson, returning for the first time after his injury in the first match, was out of touch and unhappy, and his hands let him down as well as his timing. This was sad, for he could play much better and it was Edwards who was again the star behind. Rhodesia had the wind behind them and Kiernan was made to run by the kicking Martin. The forwards were finding it difficult, especially in the front row, and the Lions were forced to defend for long periods while they rarely moved in unison.

They continued in similar style in the second-half and it was 17 minutes old before they really got cracking, and then the Lions produced some of their best fast-moving rugby to delight the friendly crowd that was so glad to see them in action. Gibson became surer of himself, and Edwards continued to weave patterns, while the back-row forwards really got to the loose ball and won possession.

Rhodesia were still fighting back and Alexander and Martin, with full-back Herman, did noble work in defence. However, they could not stem the tide for ever and twenty-one points were scored by the Lions in the last 21 minutes. On reflection I feel the selectors (as much as any one) were deceived by the match, for the play of the forwards was not tight enough to match the Springboks in the Test, and it was not likely that they would win as much good possession from the mauls.

The heavier Springboks were likely to pin down the Lions loose forwards and rob the backs of the chances to attack. This, of course, they did, but at the end of the match at Salisbury despite the injury to Keri Jones in the second-half with a pulled hamstring, the Lions were confident. Barry Bresnihan once again did his 'substitute' act for the final fifteen minutes with Jones ruled out as unfit by the local doctor. However, the final fifteen minutes of play belonged to Jarrett, who scored a try, kicked a penalty goal and two conversions to collect twelve points, after he had injured his shoulder in a tackle.

It was an interesting match, too, for John O'Shea, the Lions 'Chief Justice' who was playing in his second match. He played quite well in the loose and got two tries which must have cheered him, as well as winning him a Test place, although upon reflection it was really too early, with only two appearances, to risk him in a test against the heavier and possibly fitter Myburgh.

Referee Robertse did a good job and it was likely that his performance put him in line for a Test, for he was up with the play, and made no real error. Edwards made a lovely break after eleven minutes and Taylor and Davies combined to send Thomas galloping over for a try but Kiernan kicked wide. Martin equalised with a penalty for Rhodesia before Kiernan kicked the Lions into the lead again after twenty-three minutes.

The rest of the first-half was not outstanding with Rhodesia holding their own and they deserved to be less than three points behind at the interval. The second-half began like the first and the Lions were struggling to break out of the Rhodesian grip, until O'Shea got his first try after 17 minutes. Kiernan converted and five minutes later converted the second try by O'Shea which made the score 16–3 and pointed the way to a comfortable win for the Lions.

They went on to justify themselves when, from possession at a line-out, Gibson dropped a high thirty yard goal. In the final fifteen minutes Jarrett had his first kick at goal of the tour, a penalty attempt from a wide angle at 30 yards and he succeeded. Two more tries came, one from Jarrett and the other from Hinshelwood, and Jarrett converted both.

Rhodesia made one last effort in the final minute and Denyer and Jones paved the way for a good try by Smith in the left corner. This was lustily cheered and everyone left the ground in good heart, with all Rhodesians expressing the wish that the Lions would call again at Salisbury and enjoy themselves during the future tours!

Seventh Match – The First Test
Versus South Africa at the Loftus Versveld Ground, Pretoria, Saturday June 8.
Springboks won by two goals four penalties and one try (25) to one goal and five penalties (20).
Weather: Fine and Sunny. *Ground:* Firm and dusty. *Crowd:* 75,000 (record).
Teams:
SOUTH AFRICA: R. L. Gould; J. T. Englebrecht, E. Olivier, S. Nomis, C. Dirksen; P. Visagie, D. W. de Villiers (capt.); M. Myburg, G. Pitzer, H. Marais, F. P. du Preez, H. J. Naude, P. Greyling, T. P. Bedford (vice capt.), J. Ellis.
BRITISH ISLES: T. J. Kiernan (capt.); M. C. R. Richards, J. W. C. Turner, F. P. K. Bresnihan, K. F. Savage; B. John, G. O. Edwards, S. Millar, J. Young, J. P. O'Shea, P. K. Stagg, W. J. McBride, M. G. Doyle (vice capt.), R. B. Taylor, R. Arneil.
Referee: Mr M. Baise (Western Province).

In many ways a disappointing match as a spectacle, considering the perfect conditions and the enthusiasm of a fair-minded record crowd basking in the sunshine. Certainly a disappointment for the Lions who despite the final score of 25–20, did not achieve anything near as much as they intended. In fact they were well and truly beaten and the winning margin for the Springboks could have been much greater. It was the magnificent kicking of captain Thomas Joseph Kiernan, that kept them in the hunt, for his 17 points out of 20 was quite the best kicking performance by a Lion in a test match.

The Lions tried their hardest, of this there is no doubt, and several players, especially Gareth Edwards at scrum-half, revealed admirable courage, but the Springboks were the better side. They were better drilled and equipped for the hard and vigorous play that features test matches overseas. They knew what they wanted to achieve and how to do so. Their tactical plan was complete, efficient and relentless, and perfectly executed, while the Lions were not as efficient or able as their opponents. It was the old story of a more powerful pack getting its own way against a brave British eight, and of British backs making mistakes under pressure.

This was an all too familiar pattern for me, watching my 21st test match overseas, and although I had been more optimistic than usual, at least since the victory at Auckland in 1959, it came as no great surprise to me. The Lions pack, without Horton, Thomas and Telfer, was not quite as hard as it should have been, and the loss of Barry John at outside-half, after 15 minutes play, was irreparable. He was the one back capable of piercing the Springboks back-division, and when he left the field the remaining backs were inadequate for the task, even though they did not receive a frequent supply of good ball.

John pierced the Springboks defence in two runs and at the end of his second, when he may have run just that yard too far and checked for support, he was knocked to the ground by flank forward Ellis, falling awkwardly on his shoulder. His injury was obvious to fellow players, although the first-aid men asked him to raise his arm and swing it. He was escorted sadly from the field and with him went whatever chance the Lions had of sharing the honours or even winning.

There was a long gap of fourteen minutes before the substitute Gibson appeared but he had to change and warm-up before taking the field, a fact which raised the question of having the substitutes in track suits near the touch-line, ready for immediate service. In the case of John, the substitute should have been on the field in a couple of minutes, but these were early days of the revolutionary change and officials were not well acquainted with the system.

Then, on taking the field, Gibson, because he had played in only two matches on tour and was not in test match form, should have been played in the centre, with Turner remaining at outside-half. As Ellis said later, 'Gibson was nervous from the moment he took the field and presented us with no real problems. John had proved much more dangerous and it was sad that he was injured.' While the Lions were a man short, the Springboks kicked two penalty goals and the Lions got a try through McBride, converted by Kiernan, which was quite an achievement for seven forwards.

Another decisive feature in the match was the Lions line-out play which did not produce the results anticipated. From their first throw-in they used the abbreviated line of three and four men. The three were Young at one, McBride at two and Stagg at three, and the ball was either thrown in flat to McBride or high to Stagg who tapped back, not too accurately, to the waiting Edwards. The first few line-outs were satisfactory although the gymnastic Edwards had to be at his best to control the ball, before du Preez took up the task of marking Stagg, using his full weight and vigour to do so. The service to Edwards became more erratic as the Springboks countered and the three Springboks forwards barged through after the tap-down to hammer the Lions scrum-half. The result was a steadily decreasing amount of good ball and a reduction in the threat of a not too happy Lions back division.

The tactical situation was not grasped firmly by Kiernan or Doyle at this stage and the abbreviated line-out continued with the Springboks spoiling relentlessly, when there should have been alternation between the two and eight-man line by the Lions. At the set scrums the Lions were forced to hold on grimly as the heavier and more powerful Springbok pack sapped vital energy from their opponents. The big front-row of Myburgh, Pitzer and Marais was clean, hard and heavy and consequently Millar, Young and O'Shea were hard pressed, but they did not concede a tight head, which was quite a remarkable achievement.

Yet the superior weight and shove moved through the Lions pack to the tail of it and committed the three loose forwards to a great deal of pushing which slowed them off the sides of the scrum. This provided de Villiers and Visagie with space and time in which to move and they took advantage of it with some clever running which, with proper finishing, could have brought the Springboks another two tries.

The Lions forwards never gave up trying, but they found the mauls hard and heavy, as well as energy-sapping on the hard grounds and in the considerable heat. It was a severe test of a forward and perhaps one or two of the Lions were not able to match their more experienced opponents in such conditions.

As the pressure began to tell among the Lions pack and, similarly, eased among the Springbok eight, so did the three South African loose forwards increase their marauding efforts, and Ellis, Bedford and Greyling became more effective about the field. The fly-half Visagie had an excellent match against a committed Lions back-row and he pierced the defence on several occasions, while Nomis and Olivier in the centre were encouraged to run. Englbrecht made one try with a clever run but Dirksen was not too happy while Gould at full-back did his best, but was obviously one-footed.

The big Springbok forwards, du Preez and Naude, did extremely well and both were impressive in the tight and loose and scored a try apiece. Du Preez was the local hero of the moment at Loftus Versveld and his try, a fine individual effort in the mould of Colin Meads, was cheered to the echo, and the acclaim was well-deserved. McBride was the best of the Lions forwards, while Stagg found the intense approach a little too much for him and did not achieve all that was expected. Indeed, the absence of Horton, Thomas and Telfer, for various reasons, was unfortunate as their presence would have given the Lions pack additional hardness, if not quite matching the strength of the Springboks forwards.

Behind, Gibson was below par and Bresnihan proved a disappointment after his excellent play in the early matches. The three mid-field players were never happy under pressure. Kiernan at full-back had an excellent day and erred only once, when he stood firm instead of moving forward in an attempt to stop du Preez's bull-like charge, but the criticism of him in this instance need not be too great for it would have taken a Jenkins, a Bassett or a Terry Davies to have deviated the pounding Bok into touch outside the corner-flag, and Kiernan is not a big man.

However, his kicking was superb; and it was gratifying for him to achieve so much after being criticised for failure in the early matches. He rose to the occasion nobly as one of the few real players of class and ability on the day. He, McBride and Edwards were the Lions heroes, but as Kiernan said afterwards, 'Fancy scoring seventeen points and being on the losing side, in a test match!'

The refereeing of Mr Max Baise was a little histrionic, as at Cape Town, but he was up with the play and did as good a job as possible, in a match that was punctuated by continuous errors in handling on the part of both sides, but more so by the Lions. He had to award 25 penalty kicks and from eleven attempts at goal the Lions kicked five and the Springboks four. For only one thing can Referee Baise perhaps be criticised and that was on the possible interference on Stagg at the end of the short line, for otherwise he did a good job. It was obvious that South Africans – players, administrators and referees – were not happy about the short line, but much of its effectiveness was lost as the Lions overplayed their hand in this respect without adequate rehearsal.

The match, though producing 45 points, as did the 1955 first test at Ellis Park, fell far short of that in technical skill behind and in both attractiveness and excitement. Danie Craven thought it was one of the great test matches, but many South African critics agreed with me that it was not outstanding, even though the Springboks well-deserved their victory and were, for short periods, impressive as a fifteen-man attacking unit.

Seventy-five thousand spectators saw the teams take the field and the Springboks kick-off with the wind and sun behind them. They soon attacked and but for forward passes and poor finishing they would have scored twice in the first ten minutes, while Naude, who was to collect nine points, failed with his first penalty attempt. It was after 15 minutes play that Barry John made his long break of quite sixty yards before he checked and was tackled from behind. He landed heavily on his shoulder to break his left collar bone and was assisted from the field.

Immediately Naude landed a lovely 52 yard penalty with the ball going over off the inside of an upright when the Lions were penalised at a loose maul, and two minutes later Visagie increased the lead with a 30 yard penalty goal when Richards couldn't play the ball at the bottom of a maul.

Suddenly the Lions went away with Richards moving up the blind side and kicking over the Springboks back-line to their goal-line. Dirksen failed to clear and from the ensuing maul, McBride dashed away and over for a try which Kiernan converted, and it was much healthier for the Lions at 6–5. However, a tap-back by the Lions at a short line-out in their own '25' saw Naude charge through, gather the ball, and crash over for a try. Visagie converted easily and three vital errors had cost the Lions eleven points.

Kiernan then had two attempts at penalty goal. The first, from 47 yards after a line-out infringement, sailed wide but his second, from 26 yards after a Springbok had picked up in an offside position, presented no difficulty. In the next minute a pass was dropped in midfield and the Springboks pounced on the loose ball for Engelbrecht to make ground quickly and send inside to the supporting Visagie who put de Villiers over for a try that Visagie converted. It was now 16–8 and the Springboks were roaring away!

Gibson kicked wide with a drop at goal before Edwards ran wide from a set scrum without the ball and was followed by the Springbok defenders. They were lured into an off-side position and Kiernan kicked an easy penalty goal from the twenty-five line leaving the Springboks five points in the lead at the interval at 16–11. At this stage no member of the Lions party could feel too confident, for unless the Springboks tired there was little chance of winning, but Kiernan could emulate the Clarke effort of 1959 at Dunedin and win the match with penalty goals. Indeed, he almost did so by getting another three in the second half!

After 11 minutes play of the second half Visagie kicked a simple penalty from 25 yards when the Lions were penalised for bringing the ball down at a line-out and holding it briefly before sending it back to Edwards. After 20 minutes du Preez set off round the front of a line-out and pounded thirty yards for his try that virtually decided the match, although it was not converted by Visagie.

Leading by 22–11, there appeared no chance now for the Lions, but Kiernan kicked another penalty goal from 30 yards followed by another from 45 yards and it was 22–17. There was just a chance, against the run of play, for the Lions to succeed but it was Naude, with a giant 54-yard penalty goal, as at Christchurch in 1965, that really decided the issue. A line-out offence gave him the opportunity and the ball just cleared the bar while the crowd cheered madly. Yet there was still time for Kiernan to kick his fifth penalty goal from 30 yards, but the Lions could do no more. Edwards was hurt in mid-field but got up battered and bruised to make his famous remark about the hard ground! Jeff Young was hurt when a scrum collapsed before the end, to be carried from the field on a stretcher, and the Lions cup of woe was full. When the final whistle went the field was invaded and one could do nothing but offer sincere congratulations to the Springboks on their deserved victory. The road ahead for the Lions looked steep and difficult, for much was at fault during the afternoon.

Eighth Match
Versus North Western Cape at Danie Kuys Stadium, Upington. Wednesday June 12.
Lions won by two goals, two penalties and three tries (25) to one goal (5).
Weather: Dry and cold. *Ground:* Firm. *Crowd:* 8,000.
Teams:
N. W. CAPE: B. Basson; S. Mostert, N. Engelbrecht, J. Van Tonder, J. Fourie; G. Maree, L. Fouche; F. Hanekom, D. Heyman, N. de Jager, H. Steynberg, H. Engelbrecht J. Joubert, P. Hattingh, G. Bruwer (capt.).
BRITISH ISLES: R. B. Hiller; A. J. W. Hinshelwood, W. H. Raybould, J. W. C. Turner, K. F. Savage; C. M. H. Gibson, R. M. Young; A. L. Horton, J. Young, M. J. Coulman, P. K. Stagg, P. J. Larter, R. B. Taylor, J. W. Telfer (capt.), J. Taylor.
Referee: Mr J. P. J. Schoeman (Western Province).

The Lions wanted to do well in this match and wipe out as quickly as possible the memory of the Pretoria Test defeat. The weather was fine but extremely cold for the area, and what was most looked for was an improvement in the play of Gibson. The local opposition was not regarded by South Africans as strong, but it did extremely well and it was not until late in the match that the Lions were able to take control and exert their will upon the play. In fact the Lions started off with rather less enthusiasm than they showed in the test and they had to battle hard against a local pack that rose to the occasion. At half-time the Lions led by nine points to five and no more and, as one wag said, 'They were lucky to lead!'

They struggled on to mid-way through the second half and then as the local defence tired and as the forwards found it harder to keep pace, the Lions looked more capable and eventually finished the match by winning by 25 points to five. This in itself was a credit to the local side which had done well to hold international opponents to such a reasonable score in the first representative match ever played in the town. Critics were stern and rather forlorn in their hopes for the future of Gibson, who just could not recapture his best form.

He was indecisive and did not kick accurately, and one felt sorry for this conscientious young man struggling so desperately to live up to the reputation he had arrived with and to fill the vacancy caused by the loss of Barry John. The centres were not a great deal better. Raybould still favoured the inside dash while the three mid-field players rarely let the ball flow to the fast moving wings.

After the match Dawson was of the opinion that the field was narrow and that was why the players moved play back inside instead of outwards, but probably the loyal coach was defending his players because the field was NOT narrow. We measured it, and as Jack Horn said, 'Ach man, it is a good field!' Perhaps the side in this match lacked the discipline it developed later and was to reveal in the Second Test. They certainly needed a better pattern of play for they should have won by more than thirty points.

Critics were still comparing this Lions side with the 1955 side, and they were falling a little short at this stage. However, it is fair to report that Telfer and John Taylor had been out of the side for some time and were playing themselves back into form. Unfortunately for Taylor (surely, with Jarrett and John, the unluckiest men on the tour), he damaged his shoulder although his leg passed the test. He was to miss another three matches and began to wonder if he would ever enjoy a break!

Young worked hard as hooker and Coulman made many dashes from the line-out while completing the peel-off, and Bob Taylor also ran round smartly. Hiller hovered between his full-back position and the mid-field position in his traditional Barbarian manner and collected ten points with four place kicks. Always an entertaining player, he was still an enigma, although by this stage of the tour he had resigned himself, probably, to being second choice to Kiernan. It is always hard on tour when you are

Number Two in any position, but Hiller's loyalty was never in doubt.

The Lions took the lead after six minutes when Hinshelwood got over in the right corner as he was tackled after Coulman had peeled from a line-out, but Hiller could not convert. However, the full-back increased the lead after twenty minutes with a twenty yard penalty from an easy position. Near the interval this lead was reduced when the North West scored. They moved to the blind side of a scrum and Steynberg put Bruwer over for a try that Basson did well to convert.

The Referee in this match, Jan Schoeman, was an average official, but little did he realise then that he would get a test match, and become the centre of a raging controversy. He awarded the Lions nine penalties and the North West ten during the match, with the Lions having five kicks at goal and their opponents three.

Hiller kicked an easy penalty early in the second half after the Lions had led 9–5 at the interval because Roger Young had collected a good try just before the interval that went unconverted. From 12–5 the Lions went to 15–5 when Hiller joined the attack and Turner was able to cross in the corner. Hiller missed the conversion, only to convert the next try by Telfer, who supported a Turner burst after switching direction.

Ten minutes from the end Turner burst through, was tackled, and the Lions won the maul for Roger Young to put Gibson over for a try. This time Hiller kicked the goal. The Lions could not add to their total in the closing ten minutes of play and this was disappointing, for had they really been in form, they must have scored again, despite the valiant defence of the North West.

Ninth Match
Versus South West Africa at Windhoek. Saturday June 15.
Lions won by one goal, two penalties and four tries (23) to nil.
Weather: Really warm with breeze. *Ground:* Firm. *Crowd:* 8,000 (Record).
Teams:
S. W. AFRICA: F. Louw; H. Snyman, S. Steenkamp, A. Van Wyk, N. Smith; G. Pool, G. Fourie J. Kotze, F. Bassingthwaite, B. De Klerk, P. Swart, W. Van De Venter, J. Tromp, K. Nel, J. Ellis (capt.).
BRITISH ISLES: R. B. Hiller; K. F. Savage, F. P. K. Bresnihan, W. H. Raybould, A. J. W. Hinshelwood; C. M. H. Gibson,

G. O. Edwards; J. P. O'Shea, J. V. Pullin, M. J. Coulman,
W. D. Thomas, P. J. Larter, R. J. Arneil, J. W. Telfer (capt.),
M. G. Doyle.
Referee: Mr H. Kruger (S.W. Africa).

Since the War the Lions had always experienced hard matches
at Windhoek and mentally they were well-prepared for this one.
They realised that Jan Ellis, the Springbok flanker, playing at
No. 8, would be keen to contain the Lions halves and that there
would be an all-out offensive at forward. The weather was
extremely warm but there was a fair breeze blowing at the ground
which helped provide reasonable conditions although the ground
looked, and was, hard despite its layer of grass.

In actual fact the match turned out to be a duel between Ellis
and Edwards and it was Edwards who won it, quite easily. He
produced his best game of the tour up to that time and looked a
player of considerable skill, judgement and pace. He got two
tries and one of them was a magnificient effort from forty yards
out, in which he sold as many dummies to his own side as he did
to the opposition!

Ellis chased him all the afternoon, and this was a tactical error,
for he did not spend the time leading and driving his own forwards. Had he concentrated more on them and less on Edwards, it
would have proved more beneficial, not that the South West would
have won, because the Lions forwards under the leadership of
Telfer was much more purposeful.

The South West pack were big, heavy and vigorous at first, but
the Lions stood fast and eventually were able to contain their
opponents and win a good supply of the ball. Arneil and Telfer
were lively in the loose and as Ellis chased Edwards so did Doyle
keep an eye on Ellis. Thomas and Larter did better at the line-out
and Coulman and O'Shea were workers in the tight and loose,
while Pullin won the tight head count.

The fact that Edwards had a good supply of the ball was
important, for it allowed Gibson more time to plan his approach.
However one failed to see the full advantage of the long diagonal
kick-away from his forwards so as to tire the opposing pack.
Apparently this was a basic Lion tactic at the time, but while it
has its occasional value, I was more inclined to the kick back to
the forwards' touch-line or the high punt to commit the full-back.

Often such kicks are too far and not high enough, but with time Gibson could do this, and throughout the tour I felt it should have been used more frequently.

Gibson was always trying hard and no one could accuse him of taking things easily, but it was his judgment that was slightly at fault at this stage of the tour, and probably it was mainly as a result of his trying too hard, without having fully recovered his confidence. On the other hand, Edwards was brimful of confidence, dodging and ducking, darting and deceiving, like a magician. One delighted at seeing this young man play so well.

Hiller enjoyed himself at full-back and collected another eleven points to overtake Kiernan in the points race. Yet one could never accurately analyse the play of Hiller because he was unorthodox at full-back in the French style. He believes that full-backs should attack, even at the risk of being caught out of position occasionally. Hiller could always argue that he scored more points than he conceded.

In this match the opposition failed to score against the Lions for the first time on tour, and while they had few chances of try-getting they were awarded 13 penalty kicks and seven of them from shooting range, at least in the opinion of the South West captain, and he took five of the seven kicks at goal, alas, without success. Pool, the outside half took the other two, but Louw at full-back, who for most of the match played well, did not get a kick at goal.

Perhaps Ellis assumed too much responsibility in this match which was unfortunate, both for his side and himself. Hiller put the Lions ahead in the first minute with a thirty yard penalty goal following a penalty award at the second line-out. Then it was twenty minutes before the Lions increased their lead after drawing much of the fire from the South West pack.

Edwards went to the blind side of a 40 yard scrum and raced up the touch-line with players on both sides of him, but he sold dummies and eventually dived over himself for a sparkling try. Hiller could not convert this nor the second try by Edwards ten minutes later, when he went to the open side of a maul from 15 yards. This was followed by an Edwards dash to the blind side of a maul, then a long pass which put Raybould over for a try that Hiller did well to convert from near the touchline.

It was 14–0 at the interval and after 15 minutes of the second half, Ellis was trapped waiting offside and Hiller kicked a good 40 yard goal swinging into the breeze. It was one of his best kicks of the tour, and soon he had entered the threequarter line for Savage to race over in the corner. He tried to convert from the touchline and only just failed.

Still in the picture, Hiller registered a try to end the scoring. Raybould kicked high to the goal-line where Savage gathered and was tackled on the line by Louw. He released the ball and the watchful Hiller was up to score a try which he could not convert. It was 23 to nil when the final whistle went and the Lions were happy.

Tenth Match
Versus the Transvaal at Ellis Park, Johannesburg, Tuesday, June 18.
Transvaal won by a goal and three penalties (14) to a penalty and a try (6).
Weather: Sunny. *Ground:* Firm. *Crowd:* 43,000.
Teams:
TRANSVAAL: P. Steyn; T. du Toit, J. van der Schyff, S. Nomis, O. Nortje; J. Barnard, D. de Vos; P. Bosman, R. Barnard, B. Strydom, K. Claassen, T. Dannhauser (capt.), S. de Klerk, C. Maartens, H. Nell.
BRITISH ISLES: T. J. Kiernan (capt.); W. K. Jones, T. G. R. Davies, F. P. K. Bresnihan, K. F. Savage; C. M. H. Gibson, R. M. Young; S. Millar, J. V. Pullin, A. L. Horton, W. D. Thomas, P. J. Larter, M. G. Doyle, J. W. Telfer, R. B. Taylor.
Referee: Mr J. Stander (Transvaal).

Prior to this match the Lions had not lost at Ellis Park since the war; they had not lost a provincial match on the tour, and Transvaal were not expected to beat them. However on the day of the match two late withdrawals played some part in the defeat, for Edwards was withdrawn as a precaution to keep him fit for the Test and McBride had to stand down because of a festering finger.

However the Lions still could have won the match, had they taken all their chances, especially in the first half, but it was the first match on tour in which Lions players and the referee clashed. Roger Young was never happy putting the ball in to the scrum and could not satisfy the referee in this respect, while Pullin had equal difficulty in striking in a manner to satisfy the referee. Consequently the Transvaal had ten kicks at penalty goal and the Lions two.

The long-range kickers of the Transvaal got three penalties and the Lions one goal in two attempts. Kiernan missed with his second shot from reasonable distance and this may well have decided the match, as it would have brought the scores level at 9 all with 15 minutes left for play. This was the real story of the match for the Transvaal played it tight with the halves, and especially the scrum-half, de Vos, kicking continually.

The Transvaal pack – vigorous from the start, with a few of its members not too particular what they did with late and short arm tackles – was held in the first half, but got better in the second and was in charge towards the close. Obviously the difficulty experienced by the Lions front-row and the scrum-half must have reduced their enthusiasm.

One reflects that in every country the touring team appears to get the worst end of the stick from referees, who always see more of their mistakes than those of the home side. This may be true when the Springboks are on tour, and it was true in this match. Either the law interpretations of South Africa were considerably different from those of the British Isles, or else the Lions were continually infringing.

One accepted that they did infringe occasionally as all sides must do, especially at the scrummage, for it is generally recognised that the laws appertaining to hooking, at the moment, cannot be fulfilled accurately and so referees if they wish can blow up every time. Again, it would appear normal for the home referee to watch the opposition, especially if the word has been spread round.

This is not an attack upon Mr Stander, who had charge of this match, or upon Mr Schoeman who followed him, in unhappy circumstances, in the next match, the Second Test at Port Elizabeth. My criticism is against the system and the International Board's method of promulgating their law amendments. They make changes which are passed to the member countries, who then prepare interpretations with the help of their Laws Sub-committees. Finally, referees associations discuss interpretations, and add their own notes. It becomes more and more involved and what started as a simple change at the Board's meeting, eventually is something quite different when enforced by referees on distant fields. It certainly has different interpretations in different countries and it is this factor that confuses touring teams but it is the referees who get the full blast of criticism.

This happens in all countries. Wallabies' Manager McLaughlin complained about the referees in Wales in 1966; manager O'Brien complained about N.Z. referees 'watching the red jerseys and not the black' during the 1966 tour; the Springboks complained about 1965 Australian referees, and now the Lions were complaining about South African referees and the All-Blacks about Australian referees. It goes on and on, and will do so until the Laws of the Game are simplified and a common interpretation enforced.

It was rather unfortunate that the Transvaal should revert back to ten-man rugby rather than move their backs because test players, Barnard at outside-half and Nomis in the centre, can run with the ball, but were given few chances. The Transvaal believed in pounding away at forward and they did so, and good fortune attended their efforts.

Their long distance kickers got them the lead after the Lions led 6–3 at the interval. They moved to 9–6 and then Kiernan failed to equalise, before a charged-down punt by Davies on his own '25' line let them in for a simple try which made the match safe. Yet, despite all their difficulties, the Lions could have won easily and made the match theirs by the interval.

It is true that the Lions faced a determined defence in mid-field and from the back-row which prevented them scoring more tries. Davies was carefully watched, as the Transvaal regarded him as the number one danger man. However Roger Young had a hard game in difficult circumstances while Savage was busy on the right-wing. Thomas went well at forward and was going better than anyone in the closing stages.

Gibson put the Lions in the lead after four minutes when he stood deep at a five yard scrum and feinted to drop at goal before moving left and dancing through for a try. Kiernan failed with the conversion.

After 22 minutes play Kiernan kicked a lovely penalty from 42 yards and the Lions were moving steadily into what could have been a commanding lead. Then full-back Steyn kicked a 55 yard penalty for the Transvaal and the battle was on, for it was just a taste of their long-distance kickers. It is true that the Lions kept attacking until the interval without achieving any more points.

After 10 minutes of the second half, du Toit on the wing took a hand at the place-kicking and landed a thirty yard goal to level the scores. After 24 minutes the Transvaal captain, Dannhauser, kicked his side into the lead with their third penalty goal from 55 yards. Next came the chance for Kiernan and he kicked wide from the '25' line. The last chance had come and gone!

Ten minutes from the end, Davies short-punted while attacking from his own '25' and the kick was charged down. Van der Schyff picked up and sent hooker Barnard pounding over for a simple try. Du Toit converted easily and the Transvaal were eight points in the lead.

They held on to it and had two more chances of increasing it as the referee maintained his grip on the game and the Lions. Dannhauser hit an upright from 60 yards and Du Toit was wide from 45 yards. The big siege guns of the Transvaal had won the match, and the Lions suffered their only provincial defeat of the tour.

Eleventh Match – The Second Test
Versus South Africa at Boete Erazmus, Port Elizabeth, Saturday, June 22.
Match drawn, each side scoring two penalty goals (6).
Weather: Warm and sunny. *Ground:* Firm. *Crowd:* 58,000.
Teams:
SOUTH AFRICA: R. L. Gould; C. W. Dirksen, E. Olivier, S. H. Nomis, J. P. Engelbrecht; P. J. Visagie, D. J. de Villiers (capt.); J. L. Myburgh, G. Pitzer, J. K. F. Marais, J. H. Ellis, F. C. Du Preez, J. P. Naude, M. J. Lourens, T. P. Bedford.
BRITISH ISLES: T. J. Kiernan (capt.); A. J. W. Hinshelwood, J. W. C. Turner, F. P. K. Bresnihan, K. F. Savage; C. M. H. Gibson, G. O. Edwards; S. Millar, J. V. Pullin, A. L. Horton, P. J. Larter, W. J. McBride, R. J. Arneil, J. W. Telfer, R. B. Taylor.
Referee: Mr J. P. J. Schoeman (Western Province).

This match produced the surprise of the tour and became one of the most controversial. What happened before it and during it, echoed through the corridors of rugby power in both countries for many a day afterwards. Perhaps this was a good thing for the game, generally, for it exposed many weaknesses in its set-up, but it left one man, the Referee Mr J. F. J. Schoeman, more exposed than any one, and yet he was not really the 'culprit' for no one person was the culprit in the controversy that followed, but the Game's administration at top level in all countries.

The Lions shared a draw, which was out of keeping with pre-match forecasts, but they deserved it because of their superhuman defence, which was the best displayed by a Lions side in any country since the war. To state that it was truly magnificent in every way, well-marshalled as a unit, brave individually, and decisive near the scrum and line-out, is still not praise enough. It was 'Verdun', a 'Mons', a 'Battle of Britain', for the Lions held; yes, the thin 'red line' held against long periods of siege by a determined South African side which won quite seventy per cent of the possession.

The match was hard and unrelenting but apart from a flagrant punch on Gibson which apparently was meant for someone else – this was a clean but hard match. It was exciting only in the closing stages as the Lions, having drawn level, defended desperately against constant Springbok attacks. The tackling was superb and the Springboks just could not score.

As I have said, the Springboks won at least 70 per cent of possession, and this was vital since it enabled them to control play and deny the ball to the Lions, who rarely had a chance to attack. However, a few well-placed high punts worried Gould at full-back and the Lions were able to attack for brief periods in the Springboks' '25', but there was nothing persistent in these attacks for the Springboks would always win the ball and drive the Lions back.

The Lions complaint about all this was that they were afraid to go for the ball in the set scrums, even on their own loose head, and they found the line-out law interpretation difficult to over-come. The British Press had ample proof of this in that one of their number ran the touch-line taking photographs and he returned to the Press Box at the end of the match saying that he had never before seen such unusual refereeing!

Immediately after the match Manager Brooks made a statement to the same pressman saying, 'We are terribly disappointed with the standard of refereeing in the match and thought the fact that a Springbok forward could double-rank continuously at the line-out, was disgraceful'. It is true that Brooks said this in the heat of the moment but, later in the evening, he confirmed this to half a dozen British pressmen. He said a number of other things and was supported by members of the team. On Sunday morning he gave a long, official interview to Paul Irwin of the *Rand Daily Mail*, and while he may not have complained officially about it to the S.A. Board, I know that he spoke to Doctor Craven about it.

The main complaints were that everytime Pullin struck he was virtually penalised and Edwards was unhappy whenever he put the ball in. Consequently Edwards became afraid to put the ball in other than extremely slowly and Pullin was afraid to strike. Syd Millar, senior member of the Lions front-row, gave the order not to strike on the Lions put-in, but to get down as low as possible and shove hard in an attempt to slow down the inevitable Springbok heel. All this was a considerable disadvantage to the Lions, causing Manager Brooks to make a statement later, 'How are we going to WIN the ball in the set scrums, if we cannot strike?'

The next complaint was that at the front of the line, a Springbok forward was allowed to stand out of the line (in a double-banking position) to support his jumpers. He was not penalised once and this was contrary to the laws of the game. There were other things, such as the not allowing of three 'marks' by Lions and one by a Springbok, while the second half penalty goals scored by both sides, should, in my opinion, not strictly have been awarded. So it was a tale of woe, but Referee Schoeman was more to be pitied than blamed, for he should, I feel, never have been given the match.

The S.A. Board could have proved themselves more generous and given the Lions the man they requested, Walter Lane, and they would then have been in the clear; win or lose, the Lions would have had no complaints.

The famous 'week after' is described in the Diary section of this book and I will therefore return to the actual play in the match. After all, that is what nearly sixty thousand watched with absorbing interest, even though the end left them a little in the air and without complete satisfaction. A draw is never really satisfying, but the British received a boost from it. They had held the Springboks

and it would be on TV at home on the following Tuesday, for all
to see how it was done.

By hard tackling; the keeping of cool heads under pressure and
a remarkable performance by Tom Kiernan at full-back. He gave
the best display of his career, for I cannot recall him playing
better. Kiernan kicked magnificently in the First Test to keep his
team in the hunt, and that was the best place-kicking sequence by
a Lion in a Test since the war from the full-back position. In
this match he gave the best technical exposition, or at least one
every bit as good as Terry Davies in New Zealand in 1959, and
that is high praise!

He took the high punts beautifully and made a few superb
marks in face of charging Springboks and never winced. His
tackling, too, was splendid and one made head-on, of Dirksen,
saved a certain try. The Springboks just couldn't catch him out
of position. Tom was 'tops' on this warm day at Port Elizabeth
and justified all the faith placed in him by the four Home Unions
selectors.

The whole threequarter line tackled like demons and darted
away with the few chances they had in attack. Bresnihan and
Turner crashed their opponents to earth and were up again, before one could say 'tackle', to bring down another attacker. This
was the quickest recovery 'act' ever produced by a Lions defence
and it earned them the draw.

Gibson was much steadier and did his fair share of tackling,
falling, and clearing to touch while Edwards, despite the lack of
possession and difficulty with the referee, was here, there and
everywhere, and made several brave attempts to run the Lions out
of trouble. 'It is much harder than an international at home, but
the Springboks are not dirty, although they play so hard. After
being under a maul here, you know you have been in a rugby
match!' Without having experienced it, I can only endorse the
remarks of the courageous young Edwards, while watching from
the Press Box!

The Lions forwards stuck at it and the back row of Arneil,
Telfer and Taylor tackled and covered, tackled and covered, and
pushed and fell, until they had hardly a leg under them, but they
survived tenaciously. McBride was a tower of strength at the line-
out and in the tight-loose play, while Larter did well in his first
test and gave it all he had. The front-row stood up well to the

pressure even though reluctant to strike and the Lions had every right to feel proud of themselves after 80 minutes of hard, battling football.

The Springboks must have felt disappointed, for they had their chances and failed to make full use of them, being thwarted, mainly, as a result of the stern Lions' tackling. The forwards though never able to break out and dominate, worked hard to win the ball from tight and loose. Naude did well at the line-out, and their mauling in the loose won them most of the ball. Bedford again proved a sound leader, and on this showing I would have preferred him to de Villiers as captain of the side. However, it was pointed out to me that he was 'English speaking', and would not be popular with a mainly Afrikaans-speaking side. My answer to this was, 'He's making a jolly good job of leading the pack! '

It was at half-back that the Springboks appeared to falter and again at threequarter where they had no really elusive runner. De Villiers at scrum-half was badly shaken early in the match and his running and timing never reached top standard although he tried hard. Visagie played it straight, up and down field, mainly kicking or handing straight on, and he was predictable. This time, however, his place kicking form failed to match that of Pretoria and so suffered much adverse comment from South African critics after the match; not all of it deserved I am afraid, but there was a large school of critics and followers who preferred the more elusive Jan Barnard of the Transvaal at fly-half.

It was suggested that Visagie move to full-back where he would be more useful, and also because Gould was a one footed kicker in the position. However, I thought that Gould, apart from three occasions when a kick ahead troubled him, played quite well. He was harshly penalised in the second-half, and played as well as any of the backs. Dirksen had several chances but could do nothing but run straight while Nomis and Olivier never evaded the Lions tackling in the centre.

The best thing the Springboks did in this match was to move left, win the ruck, move right and stretch the defence, win another ruck and then move left again, and menace. I can only say that the Lions did a wonderful job eventually to hold this magnificent modern movement which could have been the match winner.

It was in the second half, and had the Springboks scored then they would have won the match. Bravo the defenders in Red! Kiernan kicked the Lions into the lead after 12 minutes with a penalty goal from 30 yards after the Springboks got off-side at a maul. After 32 minutes Visagie equalised when Pullin was penalised for 'crouching' 35 yards out. After eight minutes of the second half Telfer fell off-side and Naude kicked a 30-yard penalty. Finally, after 21 minutes, Gould was penalised for holding the ball on the ground and Kiernan kicked a straight 22 yard goal. No more points were scored and the teams retired in silence, for there was no one for the large crowd to cheer. The Lions deserved some applause!

Twelfth Match
Versus Eastern Transvaal at Springs, Saturday, June 29.
Lions won by five goals, two dropped goals, one penalty and one try (37) to one penalty and two tries (9).
Weather: Dry and sunny.   *Ground:* Hard and yellow   *Crowd:* 25,000.
Teams:
EASTERN TRANSVAAL: B. Mulder; H. Thorn, B. Hirt, J. Esterhuizen, K. Cronje; O. Stumpke, R. Hector; J. Van Huysteen, K. Burger, T. Kruger, J. Brits, I. Olie, N. McIntyre, O. Jacobson, P. Wilkinson.
BRITISH ISLES: R. B. Hiller; A. J. W. Hinshelwood, W. H. Raybould, T. G. R. Davies, M. C. Richards; C. M. H. Gibson, R. M. Young; M. J. Coulman, J. Young, J. P. O'Shea, P. K. Stagg, W. D. Thomas, M. G. M. Doyle, K. Goodall, R. B. Taylor (capt.).
Referee: Mr R. Woolley (Springs).

Some days on tour you receive a premonition that something is going to happen, for no good reason at all. This must have been just one of those days. My trip from Johannesburg to Springs was most enjoyable, with three laughs a minute, but the trouble started when the cars entered the V.I.P. park, since someone then backed into Vivian's car, as detailed in the Diary Section of this book. From then on the action was fast and furious!

The match got off to a good start, with the front-rows 'working on' each other in the early set scrums. Yet it was never difficult for the Lions who were 18–6 up at the interval. They increased the lead to 23–6 before O'Shea was ordered off, and the Tour reached its climax from a news angle. Then the rugby flew over the stand and away to the high veld, stopping we knew not where, but fortunately at Loftus Versveld as later events proved.

All the writing, talking and typing was about the 'Battle Of Springs' but, fortunately, the Lions ripped into top gear and collected another 14 points which indicated that but for the 'flare-ups' and the sending-off, the match would have been remembered as an outstanding performance.

The Lions searched for the ball after getting quickly to the break down. They rucked and heeled smartly and Young at scrum half was able to supply Gibson with a stream of good passes. What is more important, the outside-half ran on to them at top speed and then varied his play well. This was the Gibson we had waited so long to see; the confident player. If lacking the cheekiness and extra elusiveness of Morgan and Watkins, he was now living up to the standard of a really good Lions outside-half.

After watching nearly 150 Lions matches, one gets to expect the best in each position and is able to compare many great players. The pleasure of a Lions tour is that of always watching what are virtually the best rugby players in the British Isles in action. They set their own standards and only the best is recognised. Since the war there have been Kyle, Cleaver, Preece, Morgan, Baker, Risman, Waddell, Sharp, Watkins, John and Gibson and, of these, some were greater than others.

The most successful were Morgan and Risman, probably because they were able to survive and take advantage of the fact they were in slightly better sides. Gibson's one handicap was that he took a long time to reach his best form on any tour. Whereas most of the others were soon as good, if not better, than they were at home, Gibson did not come good until the second half of this tour, and then faded again before the end. A fact made all the more unfortunate by the sad injury to John, who might have been more effective than Gibson, had he remained fit.

Davies returned to something like his best form in this match and ran through the Eastern Transvaal, after the 'incident', at great speed, while Richards got one classic try with the turn into the full-back, and the move away again for the corner. When he received the pass he was in a position to be tackled and it takes a good wing to score under such circumstances.

Hiller at full-back, enjoyed himself, for he loves to play football, but not for him the dour, serious stuff. His shrewd and subtle sense of humour permeates his play on the field; sometimes with considerable success and other times with alarm and concern! Not to be outdone by his captain he collected 13 points with six kicks. The accuracy of the two full-backs was quite phenomenal in Lions history, and easily the best since 1959 when Davies, Hewitt, Scotland and Thomas were all place kickers of quality.

But it was the forwards who did well, even when reduced to seven in number for almost the last half hour of the match. Coulman ran well from the line-out and maul; Young hooked four tight heads against one and Thomas, Stagg and Goodall won much possession at the line-out.

When O'Shea left, Delme Thomas went up to prop, as he had done in New Zealand in a test match. Bob Taylor as captain was excellent in fluid play and at the end of the line-out, while being fitter, he applied much more shove to the set scrums.

Obviously Springs were a bit 'niggly' from the start at forward, and one of the flankers appeared to me a little more than lively. Roger Young, at scrum half, did not enjoy some of the treatment he received. Naturally the Lions retaliated, but not Young, who is one of the game's most likeable characters, and it was his many friends in the team that protected him, readily. I understand the Springs' player concerned was recalled for this match, and dropped immediately afterwards. Had he been sent off with O'Shea, justice would, in my opinion, have been done, but it was not altogether Referee Woolley's fault.

As the 'battle' warmed, Referee Woolley tried to encourage some of the players on both sides to play rugby. Perhaps he was not quite strict enough at the start, but later he told me that he issued a general warning, and especially to the two front rows, that the next player to swing a punch would be sent off. Then after eleven minutes of the second half, it happened!

A scrum broke up as Eastern Transvaal were awarded a penalty kick fifteen yards from the Lions goal line. It seemed that a knee was put into Roger Young, once again, and then the hooker, Burger, appeared to swing a punch at O'Shea, as can be seen on the TV film. This infuriated O'Shea who chased after Eastern players swinging punches. Other players joined in. While this was going on, Hector, the E.T. scrum half, had taken a short penalty and hared away for the Lions goal-line. He bumped into one of his own players in front of him, on the way to the line, but he got over and was awarded the try.

As Referee Woolley turned round to run out for the conversion, he had his first glimpse of the 'troubles' and saw O'Shea swinging a punch and being involved with two or three E.T. forwards by this time. Woolley ran to O'Shea, broke up the fighting and then ordered O'Shea to the touch-line. He had acted on what he had seen, and however sad it was for O'Shea, one must admire Referee Woolley for having the courage of his convictions. As Ace Parker suggested later, 'It could save the tour!'

O'Shea, naturally, was reluctant to leave, for it is a terrible thing to have to walk off the field, alone and unwanted. Colin Meads did it at Murrayfield amidst a hushed silence, but here at Springs the crowd booed and pelted the unfortunate Welshman with oranges, apples, cushions, etc., as he walked along the touch-line to be met by two close friends in prop, Tony Horton, and assistant manager, Ronnie Dawson. It was sad for O'Shea and the team because he was their popular 'judge', and at that moment it was easy to see why the All-Blacks became so upset when Meads was sent off by a neutral referee at Murrayfield. However, the Lions management acted perfectly, with calm sense and dignity, although certain spectators lost control of themselves.

As O'Shea and friendly escorts reached the mouth of the tunnel, bang, a spectator leapt to the gate and punched O'Shea full on the side of the face! This was the spark that set the situation alight. In a split second, several spectators from both 'camps' were in action. Willie John McBride was first there and a right-cross virtually stopped the spectator in his tracks; the police managed to stop McBride applying the K.O., although he did well to follow up with his left! Rodger Arneil, of the gentle nature, was quickly in the melée and former British Lion flanker, now in Johannesburg, Haydn Morgan, revealed that he had lost none of his speed in getting to the 'scene of the breakdown'! Dawson did his stuff, too, and eventually O'Shea was able to get into the dressing rooms, while police, now moving from all corners to the scene, dispersed the gathering. Meanwhile, play went along merrily, as if nothing had happened, with the Lions playing even better rugby, running and handling like men inspired. They moved on to their largest win of the tour!

Poor John O'Shea was a little sad in the showers, and especially when the other 14 players joined him, but like the sportsman he is, he went straight to Referee Woolley and apologised. For the referee it was not easy, for he had sent a Welsh international off the field (the majority of people thought he was the first Lion to 'walk'), and in the 1950's, Woolley had managed a Transvaal High Schools team in Wales. It was not easy, but I am glad, as were all the party, that Kiernan, the irrepressible diplomat and laughing cavalier from Cork, praised the referee for having the courage of his convictions, at the after-match reception, at which the Prime Minister, Mr John Vorster, was a guest.

The Lions lost nothing by the manner in which they accepted the 'sending off' and, wisely, they worked hard throughout the evening, as did S.A. Board representative, Jack 'Will Fly' Horn, to ease the burden for O'Shea. They succeeded, even though all the Sunday papers in South Africa and Britain, gave the incident a 'show'.

By Monday breakfast time O'Shea had been 'reprieved' and was a happy man again! (see Diary section). The Lions moved on to Pretoria, where they were to achieve great things and where the Tour got back on to the 'main line' again for excitement and good football.

Against Eastern Transvaal, R. B. Taylor, Gibson, R. M. Young, Doyle, Richards and Davies scored tries for the Lions; Hiller kicked five conversions and one penalty and Gibson dropped two goals. Their opponents got two tries through Cronje and Hector, and a penalty goal by Nel who came on as a replacement for the injured centre Easterhuizen, early in the match. Thus Nel became the first official replacement in South African rugby history.

Thirteenth Match
Versus Northern Transvaal at Loftus Versveld, Pretoria, Wednesday, July 3.
Lions won by two goals and four penalties (22) to two goals, one dropped, one penalty and one try (19).
Weather: Warm and sunny. *Ground:* Firm and yellow. *Crowd:* 60,000.
Teams:
NORTHERN TRANSVAAL: D. Pretorious; K. Meiring, M. Neuhoff,

PLATE 36. *Left:* The master kicker. Lions captain Tom Kiernan kicks his second penalty goal in the Fourth and Final Test at Ellis Park. This kick brought his total for the series to 35 points, and a new record for a test series in South Africa. Note the perfect execution of the kick: head down and follow through

PLATE 37. *Below:* The 'big boot' of the Springbok team: Tiny Naude, the second row lock who kicked long-range penalties in the First, Second and Third Tests, at vital stages in each

PLATE 38. Dawie de Villiers (9) goes over for a try in the Fourth Test, but it is not allowed. Tommy Bedford, the Springbok pack leader, jumps over his captain in joy as R. B. Taylor, T. Lourens and P. K. Stagg race up

PLATE 39. *Left:* The try that set the Springboks in motion in the Fourth Test. Francois Roux, the Springbok centre (12), gets over for a try after a piercing run in the first half. He loses his pants as he is tackled by a Lion defender!

J. Flemix, C. Dirksen; P. Steyn, P. Uys (capt.); J. L. Myburgh,
G. Pitzer, R. Potgeiter, O. du Pitsanie, J. J. Spies, F. C. du
Preez, T. Lourens, F. du Preez.
BRITISH ISLES: T. J. Kiernan (capt.); K. F. Savage, T. G. R.
Davies, F. P. K. Bresnihan, M. C. R. Richards; C. M. H.
Gibson, R. M. Young; J. P. O'Shea, J. V. Pullin, M. J. Coulman,
P. K. Stagg, P. F. Larter, R. J. Arneil, J. W. Telfer and R. B.
Taylor.
Referee: M. W. Odendaal (Pretoria).

It is said that 13 is an unlucky number, but I am not so sure!
Manager David Brooks certainly regards it as his lucky one. The
Lions wanted to win this match more than any other outside the
tests – it was regarded, and rightly so, as the 'fifth' test. No touring side had succeeded against the Northern Transvaal for eight
years – not since the All-Blacks of 1960 – and the Lions faced a
formidable task. Yet Manager Brooks' lucky thirteen held good
for it was the 13th match of the tour and won by the Lions after
they appeared to be in for the biggest hiding of the trip, when
trailing 13–5 in the first half.

Their fighting recovery was one of the best efforts of the tour
and earned for them not only the admiration and praise of South
African critics, but most of the 60,000 spectators present and
most of the population of the Republic. In the Northern Transvaal,
they measure sport and sportsmen by the success achieved. They
felt they could win – and indeed they had a side good enough,
with a formidable pack of forwards, to have mastered the Lions.
However, they reckoned without British tenacity and courage,
which is all too rarely in evidence in these troubled times.

It is a match I will remember always: one whose final six
minutes of exciting injury time made the fingers tremble! It was
a credit to the game and lifted the tour right out of the doldrums.
It was a tour-saver that brought credit to both sides, with Loftus
Versveld becoming a name to be revered in Ireland.

Thomas John Kiernan, the Cork accountant, is normally a
quiet man, not given to extrovertism, despite the twinkle in his
eye and the happy smile. Yet he allowed himself some jollification
after this remarkable victory. Even if he had not been a beloved
leader before this match, he would have been afterwards, for he
inspired his side with six attempts at goal, all of which he kicked.
His tally of 16 points, one short of his test total of 17 a few weeks

F

earlier, gave him 33 points in two matches on the same ground on one tour, and no Lion has ever bettered this.

He suddenly became the Irish 'wizard', and as Merlin once controlled Arthur and Camelot with his magic, so did Kiernan and the 'little people' control the destiny of the Lions. It was no longer the 'Big Boot' of Don Clarke for New Zealand, but the accurate, or as my father-in-law used to say, the 'educated' boot of Kiernan, for the Lions. Yet this success left him simply, plain Thomas John, without any increase in the size of hat, but merely a determination to continue to do well for his side, whether it be his club, his province, his country or the British Lions.

Tom Kiernan, by his displays against South Africa in the first two tests, and then against the Northerns, moved himself into the select bracket of great full-backs. Terry Davies would have enjoyed Kiernan and now the pair can be classed as two of the greatest British players in the position since the war. Outstanding players always thrill; Kiernan has the true touch of rugby magic, and his name will remain honoured in the record books.

Yet Kiernan could not win this match on his own, and he had good fellows to help him. The Welsh-Irishman, John Patrick O'Shea, from the valleys of Gwent was at prop and eager to erase the dark cloud of Springs that hung over his head. When the match was over and Kiernan asked him to lead the Lions off the field, all was well. In one moment, O'Shea was a free man, a blood-brother again, for he, too, had won his stripes.

Pullin and Coulman were with him in front, battling against the superior weight of the Northerns' massive front row. They did not buckle under pressure but were often forced to give ground. During one period early in the second half, the Northerns pushed so well that Pullin just could not reach the ball on his side's put in. Coulman scored the decisive try for the Lions, from a line-out peel-off ten yards from the Northerns line. This was a try to score, against the odds, and it eventually won him a place in the Third test side.

Stagg played hard and revealed a fiery spirit that few thought existed, while the quiet Larter proved a hard man. The back-row was tireless; it had to be, and Jim Telfer held his men together when the Northerns blue tide was running hardest against the Lions in front. Then he got a crack in the face and was carried from the field, bleeding like a stuck pig. Everyone thought he was finished. Substitute Delme Thomas, standing by, went down to change, but ten minutes later the pride of Melrose returned, and drove his men to a grandstand finish.

Taylor and Arneil, like the rest of them, ran and tackled and fell, and the Northerns had spent their effort by mid-way through the second half; from 16–8 down the score changed to 16–16. Kiernan kicked two more and it was 22–16. The Lions just couldn't lose so it seemed – but a penalty to Northerns made it 22–19. Then in injury time another penalty was awarded against the Lions for wasting time. A goal was 'on'; but Pretorious missed from 35 yards and the final whistle left Kiernan's men especially delighted, and the new Kings of the North!

What of the backs? Young was brave and strong and held on like a boxer at the ropes during the first half, as his forwards were mauled, but once the pressure eased he was scurrying here and there, and feeding Gibson. The outside-half had his best match of the tour, and his tactical kicking and saving were outstanding. Back over his forwards heads would go the ball, as he found safe touches and when, in the second half, the Lions frequently employed the 'mini' line-out, Gibson was eager to move his forwards on.

By then the Northerns had lost much of their initial, all-consuming drive, and the Lions forwards moved more readily. The three-quarters defended well and the wings tried really hard. It was a team victory that surprised everyone.

Richards scored in the second minute for the Lions and Kiernan kicked an easy goal, but for the next half hour it was all Northerns and how well they played. No All-Blacks pack ever looked better, for their forwards did all things well. The score was soon 13–5 and Fourie Du Preez, a powerful attacking No. 8, got two of the three tries scored.

The Lions appeared overwhelmed but then Kiernan kicked his first penalty and it was 13–8. Near the interval a Steyn dropped goal made it 16–8 to suggest little chance of a Lions victory. The Coulman peel-off and try was the necessary tonic early in the second half and as Kiernan converted, it was only 16–13. There was a chance, after all.

The defensive period of the second half, during which Telfer was hurt and treated, appeared to take more out of the Northerns attacking than it did the Lions defending. No further scores came until Kiernan, with his second penalty, put the Lions level, then five minutes later ahead, and still further ahead after 34 minutes. Pretorious kicked a fifty-yard penalty for the Northerns, and there was exciting stuff right through injury time.

Scorers for N.T. were Fourie du Preez two tries, Pitzer one, Pretorious two conversions and one penalty, and Steyn one dropped goal. For the Lions Richards and Coulman got tries and Kiernan kicked two conversions and four penalties.

Fourteenth Match
Versus Griqualand West at De Beers Stadium, Kimberley, Saturday, July 6.
Lions won by one goal, a penalty and a try (11) to a penalty (3).
Weather: Sunny and cold.   *Ground:* Hard and yellow.   *Crowd:* 10,000.
Teams:
GRIQUALAND WEST: J. D. Smith; M. Steyn, F. Roux (capt.), J. Waldeck; E. Theron; P. Visagie, G. Swanepeol; F. Nel, H. Callaghan, A. Nel, P. Smith, W. Tolmay, J. J. Kruger, J. Markram, D. Vorster.
BRITISH ISLES: T. J. Kiernan (capt.); A. J. W. Hinshelwood, K. S. Jarrett, J. W. C. Turner, M. C. R. Richards; C. M. H. Gibson, G. Edwards; A. L. Horton, J. Young, M. J. Coulman, W. J. McBride, W. D. Thomas, J. Taylor, P. F. Larter, R. B. Taylor.
Referee: Mr K. Weyer (Kimberley).

Following the success at Pretoria, one felt there was bound to be an anti-climax immediately afterwards in the next match, and there was! This match against the Griquas was probably the most disappointing provincial game of the tour. The Lions won seventy per cent of the ball and scored two tries, both of them by the brilliant Gareth Edwards.

Perhaps the side won too much good possession, since in such circumstances it often happens that this is not used wisely, as players realise they will get further chances as the match progresses. Sometimes too much ball is a handicap greater than too little possession, and however 'Irish' this may appear to the reader, it is true. It was certainly true of the Lions in this match.

They were up against a hard side, well-coached by Springbok selector Ian Kirkpatrick, but a side that could not win possession or really challenge. Thomas, McBride and Larter dominated the line-out and Jeffrey Young won the tight head count comfortably. Again, the Lions got much good ball from the loose, and Edwards was a live wire at scrum half, but there was never close harmony in the running of the backs.

Gibson ran well on several occasions but there was not enough pace and thrust in the centre where Jarrett was returning to the side after a long lay-off and was short of match practice. Gibson was hurt in a hard tackle by Roux and Turner had a bang on the knee, but where the midfield players went wrong was that they failed to bring the wings into action regularly. This was a fault throughout the tour and, and as in other matches, too great an attempt was made to crash through in midfield rather than stretch the defence first before returning play to midfield.

Richards and Hinshelwood had the pace and skill, but were sadly neglected apart from throwing in from touch, which was fairly frequently! The Griquas had few chances to run with the ball, but enough attempts at penalty goal to have won the match. Indeed, the only Griquas score was a penalty goal at the sixth attempt by Springbok outside-half, Visagie. Neither Kiernan nor Jarrett in this match were really accurate with their kicking and only one penalty goal was achieved in seven attempts.

Thus it was a below-standard match and left little impression upon the supporters of both sides. It was clean and many of the knocks suffered were due to hard tackles on the bone-hard ground. It was said to be the hardest in Southern Africa for first-class rugby and no Lion was prepared to dispute the claim!

The one outstanding player was Edwards who sparkled like the diamonds said to be below the playing pitch. Although he may have run himself rather too frequently, without two of his best touches the Lions would not have scored a single try. He scored both of them, the first with a wide swoop and dart up the blind-side, and the second by stealing a Griquas heel from a set scrum five yards out and darting over before anyone on either side could say 'Gareth Edwards'. In achieving these two scores he revealed his speed, skill and ability to think quickly.

Francois Roux created a special image for himself as a flying tackler when he toured with Avril Malan's side in 1960–61. He caused much damage among opponents before crashing into the firm shoulder of Terry Davies at Stradey Park, from which he took some time to recover. Then in 1962 he figured in the Sharp 'incident' at Pretoria, before playing extremely well in the tests, and especially the last at Bloemfontein. He toured New Zealand in 1965 but since that year has been injury prone.

He played in this match and executed one hard tackle on Gibson, from which the outside-half took some time to recover but later Coulman cracked Roux to earth and honours were even. Off the field Roux is a most engaging, modest fellow and it was good to talk to him after the match. He did not know then but the Springbok selectors were about to recall him to the national XV, an honour he was surprised to receive.

John Taylor played in this match after a long lay-off and was delighted to come through unscathed, but for himself, Barry John, Billy Raybould and Keith Jarrett it was only half a tour, and little wonder they all wanted to go to the Argentine with Wales!

Edwards opened the scoring for the Lions after 22 minutes with his first try which Kiernan could not convert. Before the interval Kiernan kicked an easy penalty goal after the Griquas had fallen offside at a five-yard scrum. After four minutes of the second half Edwards got his second try and Jarrett converted it. There was no more scoring for half an hour before Visagie landed a penalty goal for Griquas.

Fifteenth Match
Versus Boland at Wellington on Monday, July 8.
Lions won by one goal, one penalty and two tries (14) to nil.
Weather: Sunny and warm.   *Ground:* Hard and green.   *Crowd:* 20,000.
Teams:
BOLAND: D. Visser; A. de Jong, J. Visser, C. de Jong, A. Barnard; H. Nieuwoudt, D. de Villiers (capt.); D. van der Merwe, F. du Toit, J. O'Kennedy, J. van der Merwe, J. P. Melck, D. Schoeman, K. Van Wyk, M. Jennings.
BRITISH ISLES: R. B. Hiller; K. F. Savage, T. G. R. Davies, F. P. K. Bresnihan, M. C. Richards; W. H. Raybould, G. Edwards; S. Millar (capt.), J. V. Pullin, A. L. Horton, W. J. McBride, P. K. Stagg, R. J. Arneil, P. J. Larter, J. Taylor.
Referee: D. Wege (Boland).

The Wellington ground in the wine growing area of South Africa is one of the most picturesque in the world, and the backcloth of the Drakenstein Mountains is something to be wondered at, and admired. As the weather was perfect this was an ideal setting for a match of this nature. It is true that the match did not live up to the setting, at least, not until later in the second half, but it did produce one of the wonder tries of the tour by Gerald Davies. This gave it a touch of quality, for although people may not remember the match, they will surely remember the try.

I am fond of the Wellington Ground, and always enjoy the drive out from Cape Town, as it takes one to the hills and amongst a gentle, kindly group of people. They are descendants of the oldest South Africans, the first Dutch and Huguenot settlers, and they have all the peace of mind of those brave, early peoples. The ground was packed to capacity, including the ten visiting Welshmen (actually there were seven Welshmen and three Englishmen), and the BBC TV staff high on the roof, reached by a long temporary ladder.

The Boland side was led by the reigning Springbok captain, Dawie de Villiers, and a local hero, obviously, who in this match played quite well. His forwards lacked height but not weight and strength, and they played extremely well together. They had the better shove in the scrum, and this was most noticeable while they harrassed the Lions halves, and forced them to do far too much kicking.

They made daring rushes and for periods it seemed that only Hiller was capable of keeping them out. Often the Lions were penalised under pressure but de Villiers failed with two attempts, as did full-back D. Visser. Once de Villiers refused a shot at goal almost beneath the posts and tried a tap-penalty which did not produce the anticipated try.

In many ways the match was a costly victory because six minutes from the end Edwards badly tore a hamstring, high up in his right thigh, and this ruled him out of selection for the vital third test. It was quite accidental and an indication of the risk involved to first choice test players by mid-week matches on a crowded tour. It is the same for touring teams, all over the world, but a sad feature, nevertheless.

However some poor play by the Lions was redeemed by two excellent tries, both scored in the second half, after Edwards had helped himself to a blind-side try, after 15 minutes of play, which then made him top try scorer of the tour. Hiller had kicked a penalty from 35 yards early in the second half and so the Lions led by six points to nil with 15 minutes left for play.

Then Edwards went away again and fed Savage, a greatly improved wing, who kicked on. This led to a line-out and McBride started a move in midfield before Arneil switched the attack by running wide to his right. Savage was put away again and he turned inside, then out again, before finally diving over a would-be tackler, for a fine wing's try that Hiller could not convert.

Five minutes later, the Lions moved away in midfield and Bresnihan fed Davies for the Welsh centre to burst through the middle. With two clever side steps, he slipped infield to hare for the line. He had a long way to go and the Boland side hoisted 'general chase', but they could not catch the speeding Welshman who ended up near the posts for the try of the tour, after running 55 yards. Hiller kicked an easy goal and the match was settled.

However, Boland were not done with and went near to scoring, while the final minutes were clouded by Edwards' unfortunate injury. The Lions had won another match, and at this stage their record looked quite impressive at played 15 matches, won 12, lost two and drawn one with 290 points for and 130 against. All that was needed was a victory in the Third test, and this was in the minds of all, especially the five Springbok selectors who had watched the Boland match!

Sixteenth Match – The Third Test
Versus South Africa at Newlands, Cape Town, Sat., July 13.
South Africa won by one goal two penalties (11) to two penalties (6).
Weather: Sunny and warm. *Ground:* Good condition. *Crowd:* 52,000.
Teams:
SOUTH AFRICA: R. L. Gould; S. H. Nomis, E. Olivier, F. du T. Roux, G. S. Brynard; P. J. Visagie, D. J. de Villiers (capt.); J. L. Myburgh, G. Pitzer, J. K. F. Marais, J. H. Ellis, F. C. du Preez, J. P. Naude, M. J. Lourens, T. P. Bedford.
BRITISH ISLES: T. J. Kiernan (capt.); M. C. R. Richards, J. W. C. Turner, T. G. R. Davies, K. F. Savage; C. M. H. Gibson, R. M. Young; M. J. Coulman, J. V. Pullin, A. L. Horton, P. K. Stagg, W. J. McBride, R. J. Arneil, J. W. Telfer, R. B. Taylor.
Referee: M. Baise (Western Province).

Everyone at Newlands watching the curtain raiser between the Western Province and Boland, realised that the test would be the decider. If the Lions won it they would keep the series open; if the Springboks won, the issue, with one test to play would be decided; if the match was drawn it would mean that the Springboks could not lose the series. Thus the game was the most important of the tour.

Unfortunately it also proved to be the saddest. A really sad one, for it was a match the Lions could have won had they taken their chances. Well though the forwards played, however, the backs could not rise to the occasion. Most of the 52,000 spectators who crowded the historic Newlands Ground, wished the Lions could have won, done themselves justice, and levelled the series to leave everthing for the last test at Ellis Park. Perhaps only one man was relieved at the result, and he was the Transvaal Union's secretary, Jeppe Van Heerden, who would not have been able to accommodate everyone who would have wanted to attend at Ellis Park had it been a decider!

Of all the tests I have watched overseas, this was one of the saddest. The 1959 Test at Dunedin was virtually won, and only strange interpretations of the laws, however honestly made, brought about defeat. The Second Test at Durban in 1962 had seen the Lions score a push-over try that had not been allowed, and so controversy raged after both defeats. Yet here was a defeat that no one could dispute, but just feel sad about; it was the vital defeat that changed the whole complexion of the tour.

The series was over, and although on each tour, the winning of the provincial matches is always important, they are never as vital as the winning of the test series. The Lions remained without winning a series against South Africa in the twentieth century. In the Press Box as we prepared cables for despatch, we faced the same old story...the failure of a British side to take its chances. Most tests are won on errors, and this one was no exception!

The Lions forwards played magnificently; as well as we had hoped, but the backs failed in their attacking duties. The Springboks had few chances but took them and, in the end, deserved the victory, which would never have been theirs had the Lions taken their chances. Opportunity rarely knocks twice in test rugby and the Springboks were glad enough to win.

In the first half the Lions won a good share of the ball from the set-pieces and went well in the loose, but vital chances were wasted by the backs. Once, they moved away from the loose and Gerald Davies was sent running right and diagonally. He should have gone on to the right and drawn Nomis before setting Savage free for the corner and a try. One cannot say of course that a try was a CERTAINTY, but it was the next best thing, and a great chance was lost when Davies elected to turn inside to straighten up and get trapped. So an important opportunity went abegging.

In the second half the Lions found touch in the left-corner and the Springboks, defending, put the ball back out in the same corner where the opportunist Taylor called for a quick throw in by Richards. It was a perfect throw; Taylor raised hands and head to take the ball in an unmarked position – and once the ball was in his hands, he would just have had to fall over for a try. As he lifted his head to follow the ball's flight, his eyes met the sun and he was blinded; the ball hit his hands and away, as he dived for the line a yard away.

The chance was lost and one felt dreadfully sorry for Taylor, who carried the wound for days, for no player wanted more to succeed, or the Lions to win the series. The real reason the try was lost is simple. At Newlands the new grandstand has never been completed, and at the town end of the ground there is a gap through which the sun in late afternoon, shining over the famous mountain backcloth, hits the players at a comparatively low angle. Had the stand been completed the players would have been protected and Taylor would have scored. 'Dead shot' Kiernan would have kicked the goal and the scores would have level at eight-all.

One appreciates that this is a big 'IF', but a true one and serves to emphasise the fact that British Lions are never lucky on tour. There were one or two other chances during the match when the Lions kicked rather than ran with the ball; it was a day for backs to run and the Lions did not run enough. In defence they did well, for the Springboks try was due to an error in a code number at the line-out. They tackled and kicked accurately and Kiernan was as good as ever at full-back. Yet there was something missing; some spark that could have set the Lions alight. Everyone was trying hard enough but not rising to the occasion decisively. It is difficult to apportion the blame but one felt that, however hard they played, Roger Young could have run more and Gibson should have attempted the half-break, in order to draw the Spring-bok backrow and to ease the pressure on the centres.

The pre-match tactical plan had included 'all out' attack by the centres with Gerald Davies as the spearhead. He was to be the line-breaker, but as he did not succeed except in the first-half (and then he did not send Savage away), it became necessary for the halves to attempt more and more, especially Gibson. The outside-half, who played so well against the Northern Transvaal but had not played too well in the following match, kicked strongly in this test and covered tirelessly, but did not dominate as he should have done, and did in Pretoria.

The forwards did enough to have earned victory for they were excellent at the line-out and held their own in the set scrums despite the fact that after half an hour's play, Pullin was laid out with a short right at the front of the line-out. There was no retaliation in this match or in the last test but in 1969–70, the Springbok concerned would be well advised to reconsider his approach while in the British Isles, for even British players have long memories!

The loss of Mike Coulman at prop after five minutes was a heavy blow, tactically, for the Lions, since he was the man appointed to spearhead the peel-off, and he had done it well in previous matches, even scoring a try against the Northern Transvaal. He had speed in the loose and had developed as a fine forward. Unfortunately in jumping for the ball he collided with one of his own players and fell awkwardly to the ground, tearing the ligaments round his ankle. He had to be assisted from the field.

Delme Thomas was one of the substitute forwards and 13 minutes later he appeared and took up the tight-head position, with Horton moving to the loose-head. With Pullin, the new front row did well, well enough to win selection for the Fourth Test. Thomas had played tight-head prop in the Third Test at Christchurch in 1966 and was strong in the back. He made the scrum comfortable and did noble work at the line-out especially in the short line.

Regrettably there were no peels-off to probe deep into the Springbok defences and produce a quick heel from which the Lions backs could attack more easily. There were, however, some good heels in the loose which were never properly used. Near the end, Kiernan launched a 'Garryowen' but was the only man to get up to full-back, Gould, to worry him. Had there been one more Lion in support of his captain, the equalising try may have been scored. So much for the ifs and ands; so much for the sadness and, at the end, few cheered. The Springboks had won the match and the series, but the Newlands crowd, always so sporting, appeared to be disappointed with what they had seen, and because the Lions had not clinched the match to face Ellis Park all square!

Newlands appeared full to overflowing an hour before the kick-off as the curtain-raisers delighted the spectators. Yet the figures eventually released were said to be just over fifty thousand. In the years ahead the Western Province Union must do much to improve the Newlands accomodation despite the difficulties they face, but it is THEIR ground, and the only test ground privately owned in the Republic.

Following the tragedy of Coulman's injury, the Springboks took the lead after 12 minutes, when outside-half Visagie with his second attempt, kicked an easy 25 yard penalty, after Telfer had been harshly penalised in the loose. After 35 minutes, 'Old faithful' Kiernan put one over from 20 yards and the scores were level. Ellis was trapped off-side at a maul, but the Springboks had a chance of regaining the lead as the Lions did of taking it, for both Naude and Kiernan just failed with attempts at penalty goal from the halfway. It was three-all at the interval and the Lions looked slightly the better side with an excellent chance of victory. They needed to maintain their forward momentum with support from behind and give nothing away in errors.

Two minutes after the interval, the real disaster occurred for the Lions. They called for a mini-line-out inside their own '25', and there was an error in the code number given. Poor Young was caught out of position for the clean take of the tap-back. He was trapped with the ball and forced to play it by Bedford for Lourens to gather and dash over from ten yards as he was tackled by Kiernan. It all happened so quickly and disturbed everyone. I recall saying 'Hell! ' in the Press Box, and being as near to tears as any hardened critic will ever be. Although a well-taken try, it was the turning point, for the position was too favourable for Visagie to miss the kick at goal.

Over went the kick and it was 8–3, which meant the Lions had to score twice to win. Kiernan might kick a few goals, perhaps, but it was a long road to victory. However the Lions fought back and Taylor missed his certain try, followed by a 'near-miss' by Gibson with an attempt at dropped goal. It was hard and exciting and the Lions gave it everything they had, but after 27 minutes the 'big boot' made the series safe for South Africa.

The Lions were penalised at a maul and from 50 yards Naude kicked a lovely goal to make it 11–3. Yet the Lions came back for more; eager, determined and brave, but they just could not break out for the vital scores as the Springboks defended strongly. In the 40th minutes Kiernan kicked a penalty from 30 yards and it was 11–6. Then came his 'up and under', but no more, and the match ended quietly. How much different it could have been!

Seventeenth Match
Versus Border at East London, Wednesday, July 17.
British Isles won by one goal, five penalties and two dropped goals (26) to one penalty and one try (6).
Weather: Sunny and warm. *Ground:* Firm and green. *Crowd:* 16,000.
Teams:
BORDER: L. Carstens; J. Coetzer, M. Harper, C. Du Toit, M. Dickson; B. Stickels, F. Du Plessis; B. Kretzmann, B. Harrison, J. Vos, A. Venter, A. Goosen, A. Webber (capt.), D. Coetzer, G. Preston-Thomas.
BRITISH ISLES: R. B. Hiller; A. J. W. Hinshelwood, K. S. Jarrett, F. P. K. Bresnihan, W. D. Jones; C. M. H. Gibson, R. M. Young; S. Millar, J. Young, J. P. O'Shea, P. J. Larter, W. J. McBride, B. West, J. W. Telfer (capt.), M. G. M. Doyle.
Referee: K. Carlson (East London).

One felt there was bound to be a reaction after the sad defeat of the Third Test, for it takes time even for a Lions team to recover from the loss of a series, although they must now be used to it. Again, defeat hits the senior players much harder, especially men like Kiernan, McBride and Millar, who have done a great amount of travelling in search of victory with British and Irish teams.

The Border were not regarded as an outstanding side but everyone in the Lions party realised that they would not be beaten easily. They had a tearaway pack and opportunist backs and this proved to be true. The referee was schoolmaster Ken Carlson who had disallowed the now famous push-over 'try' at Durban in the 1962 Test.

The Lions won the match, thanks to Robert Hiller at full-back, but not convincingly and it was a most disappointing day. Fortunately Hiller was in brilliant form as a kicker and once again showed what a clever footballer he is, if not the best full-back in the British Isles. He plays because he loves football, and his approach is most refreshing if not in keeping with Test match rugby.

Hiller scored 23 points out of the Lions total of 26, which was a remarkable performance. He kicked five penalties, two dropped goals and a conversion, which was only two short of Malcolm Thomas's Lions record in New Zealand in 1959. This brought Hiller's tally for the tour to 88 points in seven matches. He remained a modest, likeable fellow and an excellent tourist, who never complained at any time that he had to play second fiddle to Kiernan.

His accuracy was amazing for he started with a penalty goal after eight minutes. This was followed by another after 27 minutes and when Gibson scored a try with a fifty-yard run Hiller converted it. In the second half he started with a dropped goal after 10 minutes, another penalty after 23 minutes and a second dropped goal after half an hour. A minute later he landed a fifty yard penalty and followed this after 37 minutes with a fifth penalty from 48 yards.

The Border scored a penalty by full-back Carstens and a try by Harper, both in the second half, but the tragedy of the match was the unfortunate injury to Lions scrum-half, Roger Young. He made a blind-side break minutes from the start and was fairly tackled into touch. Unfortunately he fell over a group of schoolboys sitting within a yard of the touchline and badly injured himself, cracking two ribs.

He was carried from the field on a stretcher, but the doctor in attendance would not allow a substitute, saying he was fit enough to go on again. This he did, after Manager Brooks had said that he could retire again if in pain. Young stood it until the interval and then retired for good, where upon a 'sub' was allowed – Tom Kiernan, who also took over the captaincy from Telfer.

Young was out for the rest of the tour, Manager Brooks having to send an S.O.S. to the Four Home Unions for a replacement: Gordon Connell of Scotland. Brooks had to do this for he was without a scrum-half for the final test.

It was not a happy match, for the spirit was rather poor. The Lions were countering their disappointment and attempted to wrestle and maul with their lighter opponents, instead of making use of the good ball received. Once again they did not move play to the wings, neither did Gibson impart the steadiness needed. He was never able to control the play as a true pivot when his side was on top, and this was sad, for he had the ability, but was never able to make full used of it.

The Lions forwards did well, winning a great deal of ball; Jarrett played hard in the centre, and with few chances, it was sad that this young man was not given greater opportunity on tour. Doyle played well as an emergency scrum-half for ten minutes while Young was off the field in the first half, and was ear-marked as emergency scrum-half for the Lions against the Free State in the next match, if Connell did not arrive in time.

Although Gibson charged down a kick near the half-way to gather and run over 50 yards to score for the Lions in the first half, a good try was that scored by the Border near the end when Harper crossed. However, it was a disappointing match for the thousands of schoolboys present, and nowhere near as good as the excellent curtain-raiser between Grey College and Dale College, which produced attractive, clean fast rugby, which unfortunately the seniors could not match.

Eighteenth Match
Versus Orange Free State at Bloemfontein, Saturday, July 20. British Isles won by one penalty, one dropped, one try (9) to one penalty (3).
Weather: Warm and sunny. *Ground:* Hard and yellow. *Crowd:* 25,000.
Teams:
ORANGE FREE STATE: T. Yssel; J. Coetzee, F. de Vos, J. Jansen, M. Bekker; S. du Toit, W. Strydom; S. Van Zyl, J. Wagenaar, K. Steenekamp, P. Reineke, J. Schwartz, C. Van Zyl (capt.), T. Jordaan, J. Kleingeld.
BRITISH ISLES: T. J. Kiernan (capt.); M. C. R. Richards, T. G. R. Davies, F. P. K. Bresnihan, A. J. W. Hinshelwood; C. M. H. Gibson, G. C. Connell; S. Millar, J. V. Pullin, A. L.

Horton, P. K. Stagg, W. D. Thomas, R. J. Arneil, R. B. Taylor, B. R. West.
Referee: H. J. du Plooy (OFS).

The Free State Stadium at Bloemfontein is one of the largest in South Africa and the playing pitch is a long way from the press box because of a running track round the perimeter. The Murray-field pitch is a long way from the Press Box, as it is at Stade Colombes, but Bloemfontein is the furthest, and field glasses are necessary for the far corners, if every detail is to be high-lighted.

However, the weather is always good in winter in the city and there is a strong atmosphere of rugby football, spearheaded by the cry 'Vrystat'. Unless you have been to Llanelli in Wales, Bloemfontein or New Plymouth you have not tasted the true vigour of South African, Welsh and New Zealand rugby. I have always watched exciting matches there, even the 34–14 defeat of the Lions by the Springboks in 1962, and regret to write that this match was a considerable disappointment.

It was a scrambling, untidy game from the start with the Free State doing well in defence, harrassing the Lions, and occasionally bursting through, but with the referee, Mr du Plooy, never allow-ing the game to flow. He was, in my opinion, pedantic and over-scrupulous; the players being 'stopped in their tracks' and some-times deprived of the chance of running freely because the advantage law was nipped in the bud. It is not easy to allow a match to flow, but it must be attempted.

Again, the match was a sad one for the Lions, as it disposed of Gerald Davies, their brightest attacking centre. He was tripped after grub-kicking through, fell awkwardly to dislocate his elbow, and had to be led from the field in agony. Turner replaced him as a substitute, but Davies was lost for the final test. This was a blow, but in keeping with the Lions long list of unfortunate injuries. Against Boland it had been Edwards; then Coulman in the Third Test, followed by Roger Young against Border, and then Gerald Davies in Bloemfontein.

The Lions test hopes for Ellis Park faded with these injuries, and those of us who are able to 'read the signs' through experience, realised that it was really the end. The injuries had driven deep into the side's potential and in this match, though they won and deservedly so, the Lions were not really the side they should have been.

The match was unusual in that the Lions fielded a replacement who had arrived in Bloemfontein less that 24 hours previously. He was Gordon Connell of Scotland who had been rushed out in answer to the Manager's S.O.S. at East London on the Wednesday night. Connell left on Thursday, arrived on Friday and played on Saturday, thereby creating a new British rugby record, and beating the effort of Andrew Mulligan in New Zealand in 1959, who arrived on a Monday and played on a Wednesday.

It was a tough task for young Connell, a likeable modest fellow, who did quite well, although Referee du Plooy kept penalising him for putting the ball into the scrummage incorrectly. Towards the end of the match, having adjusted himself to the conditions and the altitude, Connell was going much better and as he walked from the field uninjured, the Management breathed a heavy sigh of relief. Injured players are the biggest nightmare of any tour, and the 1968 Lions had more than their share of misfortune in this respect.

The Free State pack were a lively bunch of forwards, their halves were opportunist, while the backs tackled sternly and chased hard. All the side got to the loose ball quickly and there were periods when the Lions had to defend stubbornly. Davies left the field after 20 minutes, an incident that did not improve the tempo of the match, and then Gibson had a left-footed drop at goal disallowed, which he claimed sailed between the posts, and I believe him!

However, after 29 minutes play Kiernan kicked one of his special penalties from 47 yards to put the Lions in the lead and four minutes later Gibson dropped his goal, properly this time, straight from 35 yards after a scrum. It was therefore 6–3 to the Lions at the interval. Turner had taken the field 13 minutes after Davies had left it, the average time during the tour for substitutes to appear being from 12–14 minutes.

The first-half was not impressive as a spectacle, but early in the second there was the best move of the day. The Lions won a scrum inside the Free State half and Gibson made for the outside gap before sending the ball inside to Turner, crossing behind him. Turner went straight through and up to the full-back before sending a high pass out to his left which Richards took very well and raced over for a try. Kiernan was wide with his conversion attempt, but it was a spark of colour which could have inspired.

The Lions were penalised at a scrum shortly afterwards and Du Toit kicked a 25 yard penalty to make it 9–3. There was little else of note in the match except for the odd dropped shot at goal, a few rushes by the Free Staters, and a final drop at goal by Gibson, that sailed wide in injury time. Another provincial side had been beaten, but the Lions did not look world-beaters. They awoke in the morning to find that they were the 'worst ever behaved team' to visit South Africa, and even the Devil himself, must have said 'Offside' when he read the front page of the Johannesburg *Sunday Times*.

Nineteenth Match
Versus North Eastern Districts at Cradock, Monday, July 22.
British Isles won by five goals, three penalties and two tries (40) to two penalties one dropped and a try (12).
Weather: Warm and windy. *Ground:* Firm and dusty. *Crowd:* 5,000.
Teams:
N. E. DISTRICTS: B. Botha; A. Pienaar, L. Strauss, D. van Vuuren, W. de la Rosa; W. Weideman, W. Lourens; M. Cretchley, A. Pienaar, J. H. Marais (capt.), R. Venter, N. Barnhorn, H. Viljoen, E. Moorcraft, P. Kinghorn.
BRITISH ISLES: R. B. Hiller; A. J. W. Hinshelwood, W. H. Raybould, F. P. K. Bresnihan, K. S. Jarrett; J. W. C. Turner, G. C. Connell; J. P. O'Shea, J. Young, A. L. Horton, P. J. Larter, W. D. Thomas, M. G. M. Doyle, J. W. Telfer (capt.), J. Taylor.
Referee: D. Symington (Cape province).

This was the last provincial match of the tour against the youngest Union affiliated to the South Africa Board, and one of the kindest and nicest. The Lions were happy at Cradock, for they liked the country town and its people and they played in this match as if they were really happy. Obviously the opposition was not as strong as that of the top provinces but, led by Hannes Marais the Springbok prop, it revealed good spirit and the match was much enjoyed.

It was remarkable for the fact that the 'Bossman', Robert Hiller, notched his hundred points for the tour with another fine display of kicking. His tally in this match was 16 points with five conversions and two penalties and it was for him, as easy as shelling peas. Yet he always takes time when placing the ball and in marking his run-up to achieve perfect timing, which is the hallmark of accuracy. His head, too, is always well over the ball at the moment of impact. If he does not give as much 'beef' as Kiernan, he is excellent up to 40 yards and particularly from wide angles. He and Kiernan were invaluable to this Lions side, which never really scored as many tries as it should have done.

In this game were several players who for various reasons had played in only a few matches on tour. These included the three Welshmen Raybould, Jarrett and John Taylor. It was their last match of the tour and Jarrett impressed on the left-wing, where he played for Monmouthshire against the All-Blacks. He is a strong runner and heavy, and his corner try was an excellent one, while he kicked a difficult penalty goal into the wind.

This suggested that had he enjoyed better fortune, and not been injured in Rhodesia, he would have had a successful tour. To say he did not train is stupid rubbish, for he was as keen as anyone, and this match proved how eager he was to play. He thoroughly enjoyed his tour and who would blame any young man at the age of 20 years for enjoying himself?

Raybould found difficulty at times in adapting his elusive running to the needs of the team. He was something of an individualist and the management appeared reluctant to play him more frequently in the outside-half position. John Taylor was just unlucky, for he played against Western Province in the second match, missed five matches before playing and getting injured again, and then played in only three more. Though on the small size, like Doyle, for South African test rugby, injury prevented him from getting into a real gallop and settling down.

Yet in this match all the Lions ran with the ball for a change, and even though outside-half, Turner, occasionally kicked when he should have passed the ball in the pivot position, there was some good running and good tries, with the opposition contributing much to the spirit of the game. A strong wind blew down the ground but the Districts did not attempt to close the game up as well they might have done in the situation. The first-half was fairly even, and the Lions led only 17–9 before they jumped into top gear in the second half and scored another 23 points against three.

The scoring of the 52 points went like this – (7 mins.) Raybould a try, Hiller converted; (10) Rosa try for Districts; (12) Hiller a penalty; (15) Botha a dropped goal for Districts; (22) Taylor a try; (26) Jarrett a try; (34) van Vuuren a penalty for Districts; (37) Jarrett a penalty. Half time score: Districts 9 points. British Isles 17.

In the second half the scoring was as followed: (6) Bresnihan a try, Hiller converted; (9) Thomas a try, Hiller converted; (16) Hinshelwood a try, Hiller converted; (31) Hiller a penalty; (40) Doyle a try, Hiller converted; (41) Weideman a penalty for Districts. Final score: N. E. Districts 12 points. British Isles 40 points.

It was the largest total of the tour by the Lions and the same margin of victory as achieved at Springs, 28 points. It completed a fine provincial record in which only one match was lost, against the Transvaal, and even that one could have been won, had the Lions taken their chances in the first half.

Twentieth Match – The Fourth Test
Versus South Africa at Ellis Park, Jo'burg, Saturday, July 27.
South Africa won by two goals, two tries and a dropped goal (19) to two penalties (6).
Weather: Sunny and windy. *Ground:* Perfect. *Crowd:* 62,000.
Teams:
SOUTH AFRICA: R. L. Gould; S. H. Nomis, E. Olivier, F. du T. Roux, G. S. Brynard; P. J. Visagie, D. J. de Villiers (capt.); J. B. Neethling, G. Pitzer, J. F. K. Marais, J. H. Ellis, F. C. du Preez, J. P. Naude, M. J. Lourens, T. P. Bedford.
BRITISH ISLES: T. J. Kiernan (capt.); M. C. R. Richards, F. P. K. Bresnihan, J. W. C. Turner, K. F. Savage; C. M. H. Gibson, G. C. Connell; A. L. Horton, J. V. Pullin, W. D. Thomas, P. K. Stagg, W. J. McBride, R. J. Arneil, J. W. Telfer, R. B. Taylor.
Referee: E. A. Strasheim (Northern Transvaal).

The last test match of a series is always a difficult one for a touring side, since the team is tired and fully aware that it is the last match and that twenty four hours after walking from the field of play, the party will be shooting up into the air, bound for home. Thus it is difficult for a side to concentrate in the days before a final test, as they packing for home; getting tickets for friends, saying goodbye to hosts, and generally thinking about everything except the match in hand!

This affects all touring teams in any country and does not make matters any easier. The 1968 Lions were subject to the same pressures as their predecessors but there was a brave effort made to face the formidable task of winning the Fourth Test. The defeat at Cape Town had made the Lions sad, but they fought back bravely and survived even the unfair and rather hysterical press attacks after East London, but I feel this anti-Lions outburst did them a great deal of damage. They did not reveal how much they had been affected but they had, and while it was not the majority of South Africans who criticised them, I feel the *Sunday Times* of Johannesburg did more harm to the touring Lions with their front page story than the loss of the Test series. It is not a pleasant thing to be told that you are a member of one of 'the worst ever behaved touring teams'.

The whole question of behaviour is discussed elsewhere in this book, but I know the Lions will find it hard to forgive the journalists who 'set up' the story, or the Johannesburg *Sunday Times* for printing it. However, the story did not represent the true affection of South African rugby followers for the Lions, and it is good to know that at Bloemfontein, Cradock and Johannesburg, everyone was kind to them, and did everything to wipe out the stigma of the attack.

After arriving from Cradock, coach Dawson worked hard on his players and the team responded as best they could, but they were not the fresh lively team of a few weeks previously. Dawson did not over-coach them in these few days but in the second half of the test, the wear and tear of a long tour revealed itself and the Lions as a team could not cover and clear as they did at Port Elizabeth and Cape Town.

The first-half was fairly even, with both sides enjoying successful periods on attack, but in the second half the Lions were up against it. The Springboks had a successful ten minutes during the middle of the half and scored ten points to move the score from 9–3 to 19–3 in their favour and it was all over. The Lions did not collapse in the final stages as they did in 1962 at Bloemfontein to be overrun, but held on to lose by a margin of 13 points.

Perhaps one should not have expected them to win the last test. The result did not affect the series which had been won already by South Africa, and the Lions were well below strength through injuries. They had Delme Thomas at tight head prop in an effort to improve the line-out play and benefit from the lesson of the Third Test, when he played well in the position as substitute. They had Connell at inside half, after only eight days in the country, and Savage, who had only barely recovered from a hamstring injury, on the wing. In addition, on the day, hooker Pullin was allowed to play with a dose of 'flu.

The Lions were not able to call upon four of their outstanding attacking backs in Edwards, John, Davies and Jones, while prop Coulman, who enjoyed the running game, was also out of action. All five would have played had they been fit, especially the midfield players, since Edwards, John and Davies were more imaginative in attack than their colleagues.

One does not suggest that the Lions would have won this test had they fielded their strongest side, but it would have been a much closer affair. The Springboks played well and deserved their victory, for it was their best performance of the series, but the Lions were not as formidable as they should have been, especially behind the scrum and in the front row.

They lost the tight-head count, nine to two, and this was due as much to Pullin's illness as to the re-arranged front row. The back row was hard pressed and because of the inability to win as much possession as they should have done as a pack, the Lions back row were committed to defence, while the Springboks back row rampaged in attack. Telfer at number eight played his heart out and the two flankers, invariably tackling and moving back to cover, were played out by the end.

For the Springbok back row it was much easier, as they were generally moving forward in possession. Bedford is outstanding in South African conditions, but only a normal player in the British Isles in the heavier going. He is an excellent player on the hard grounds in getting to the break-down and starting attacks. In this he is much better than Ellis, who is a ball-carrier and strong runner. Now Bedford has proved himself as a Springbok pack-leader, he should graduate to the captaincy of the South African side, and I can think of no better player, in view of his experience, to lead the Springboks in the British Isles in 1969–70. Dawie de

Villiers is very popular with his fellows and will have had his 'European trial' in France during November.

The big men Naude, Du Preez and Marais moved well and this Springbok pack had energy and vigour, and extra mobility. It handled particularly well in the loose, and this was a striking feature of contrast between the two packs. The Lions, developed in heavy and wet conditions in the main, can rarely maintain the momentum of a handling movement for long, while the Springboks are expert at it. In this match it was really the essential difference between the two packs of forwards.

De Villiers played well without any pressure on him, while Visagie was still a straight-forward player at outside-half. He did nothing wrong but he was not creative enough, especially as he was getting good ball from the loose, which is so vital for any side wishing to attack.

In the centre Francois Roux, who becomes more interesting the more you watch him, got one excellent try, slipping between Gibson and the centres, as they failed to close a 'gap' in the first half. Nomis and Olivier also ran elusively, and suggested that with an outside-half making them run on to the ball, they would be more dangerous. Gould at full-back is an opportunist and a lucky player, for although he has a powerful left kick, and dropped a good goal in this match the rub of the green and bounce of the ball favoured him throughout the series, except when he conceded Kiernan's second penalty, rather unfortunately, at Port Elizabeth.

The Lions back division did not shine, even when it was not under pressure and, once again, was most disappointing. Although Connell managed a reasonable service when the opportunity occured, he received a much slower service from his forwards as well as a couple of back row men with the ball! In only this point can I fault the cheerful and experienced refereeing of Dr Bertie Strasheim, for I did think the Springbok back row men were a little too quick round the scrum.

Connell also did some useful defensive work and engaged in sharp left-footed kicking but such a test match must have been an ordeal for him after only eight days in the Republic. However, he is now a test player, and I am certain he will be all the better for his experience and serve Scotland well in the future.

Gibson remained a disappointment, and while there is no pleasure in continuing criticism, it must have been as sad for him as it was for his colleagues and those watching from the stand, that he could not raise his game up to test level. The one glimpse of him 'in charge' at Pretoria against the Northern Transvaal, caused many to believe he would 'come good', but in this match he did not produce his form as an attacker, when so much was needed from him.

His centres tried hard, as indeed did Gibson, to throw off their own personal shackles, but as a mid-field trio they did not impress. Turner made the odd burst, and Bresnihan just failed to hold a comparatively low scoring pass in the one good movement, but it was the slavish devotion to the kick in attack, as in the other three tests, that robbed the Lions of their real power behind.

Whether this was due to a tactical desire pre-arranged, or to the fact that the players concerned had lost confidence in their own skills as runners and attackers, I know not, but it was all so disappointing, and the side's backs never once matched the 1955 and 1959 sides. As Alf Wilson, the former Lions manager and International Board chairman of 1968 confided to me after the test, 'At least in 1959, we ran with the ball and gave the wings a chance!' This was the complete criticism of the 1968 side. They forgot to run with the ball and starved their wings and scored only one try, and that by a forward, in four tests. Tom Kiernan at full-back again had a sound match and collected the two penalties that give him the new individual record as a test match scorer in South Africa, with total of 35 points, passing Geffin's 1949 total of 32.

There was a crowd of nearly 62,000 spectators inside the ground when the teams fielded in perfect conditions and the singing of the South African national anthem was most impressive. Rhodesia's Prime Minister, Ian Smith, sat with State president, Jim Fouché, and Prime Minister John Vorster, in the enlarged glasshouse which provides the most comfortable rugby viewing in the world.

The Press Box was traditionally full, without poor Gert Koetze and no female typists, but with the faithful and amusing Sam Merwis at my elbow, typing with the speed of sound, as we battled with the cables and the coffee and sandwiches provided. The great thing about the Transvaal secretary, Jeppe Van Heerden, is that he thinks of everything, and never forgets the Press!

The Springboks set a cracking pace from the start in an effort to crush British resistance but the Lions weathered the early storms, although Brynard did cross from a tight-head scrum and was recalled. Then after 14 minutes came the breakthrough, for Roux was sent away from a maul, and dashed between Gibson and his centres as they hesitated. He raced on gathering pace and crossed the line for a fine try as tackled. Visagie kicked wide.

After 22 minutes Kiernan equalised with the first penalty attempt of the match from 28 yards, and one hoped that this would inspire the Lions. Indeed they more than held their own at this stage, before a defensive lapse, just before the interval, was turned smartly into a score by the Springboks. Bresnihan attempted a clearance and in trying for distance, miskicked and full-back Gould fielded 35 yards out and marked, and then dropped a high left-footed goal which was properly allowed. Thus at the interval the Springboks led again by six points to three.

After five minutes of the second half, the Springboks went further into the lead from a line-out which led to a maul. De Villiers got a quick heel and went to the open side where he found Ellis with him and several others. Ellis was able to dash through a gap and dive over for a try in a favourable position, but again Visagie kicked wide.

Kiernan was hurt making a tackle to prevent a score but carried on, and slowly the Springboks got on top. During a purple patch they scored twice in the course of three minutes. The watchful Bedford got first to a loose ball and sent Olivier away, for the centre to turn inside and run round the defence for a try at the posts which Visagie easily converted. Then Gibson dropped for goal when he should have run and moved the ball. From their own drop out the Springboks won possession and galloped away, Pitzer kicking high to the left. The ball bounced awkwardly for the defence but Nomis was able to gather in full stride and race away to score. Some thought Nomis was ahead of the kicker, Pitzer, but a try was awarded and Visagie converted.

There were 20 minutes to go and the Springboks led by 19–3 and surely, we thought, they will get thirty points, but the Lions held on. Bresnihan dropped a difficult scoring pass, but was at fault, as Richards had been in the first half when he lost the ball as he was tackled crossing the Springbok line. Vital errors that cost the Lions dearly.

Actually after 22 minutes, Kiernan reduced the lead with a superb penalty goal from 53 yards, a real beauty, and there was no more scoring. Players on each side dropped for goal without success and the Lions could do no more to reduce the lead. The final whistle went, and the players were engulfed by spectators. One player was marked out for special treatment, and carried shoulder high from the field, Francois Roux, who at 29 years of age, was the symbol of Springbok superiority – he ran with the ball!

APPENDIX A: MATCH RECORD OF 1968 LIONS

Played 20. Won 15. Lost 4. Drawn 1. Points for 377. Points against 181.

No.	Date	Opposition	Venue	Result	Points for				Points against				For	Agst
					G	P	T	DG	G	P	T	DG		
1	May 18	Western Transvaal	Pot'stroom	Won	1	2	3	–	–	4	–	–	20	12
2	May 22	Western Province	Cape Town	Won	2	–	1	–	–	1	1	–	10	6
3	May 25	South West Dist.	Mossell Bay	Won	3	2	1	–	2	–	–	–	24	6
4	May 29	Eastern Province	Port Elizabeth	Won	1	3	1	2	1	3	–	–	23	14
5	June 1	Natal	Durban	Won	1	1	3	–	1	–	1	–	17	5
6	June 3	Rhodesia	Salisbury	Won	4	2	1	1	–	1	1	–	32	6
7	June 8	SOUTH AFRICA (1)	Pretoria	Lost	1	5	–	–	2	4	1	–	20	25
8	June 12	North West Cape	Upington	Won	2	2	3	–	1	–	–	–	25	5
9	June 15	South West Africa	Windhoek	Won	1	2	4	–	–	–	–	–	23	0
10	June 18	Transvaal	Johannesburg	Lost	–	1	1	–	1	3	–	–	6	14
11	June 22	SOUTH AFRICA (2)	Port Elizabeth	Draw	–	2	1	–	–	2	–	–	6	6
12	June 29	Eastern Transvaal	Springs	Won	5	1	1	2	–	1	2	–	37	9
13	July 3	Northern Transvaal	Pretoria	Won	2	4	–	–	2	1	1	1	22	19
14	July 6	Griqualand West	Kimberley	Won	1	1	1	–	–	1	–	–	11	3
15	July 8	Boland	Wellington	Won	1	1	2	–	–	–	–	–	14	0
16	July 13	SOUTH AFRICA (3)	Cape Town	Lost	1	2	–	–	1	2	–	–	6	11
17	July 17	Border	East London	Won	1	5	–	2	–	1	1	–	26	6
18	July 20	O.F.S.	Bloemfontein	Won	–	1	1	1	–	1	–	–	9	3
19	July 22	North East Cape	Cradock	Won	5	3	2	–	–	2	1	1	40	12
20	July 27	SOUTH AFRICA (4)	Ellis Park	Lost	–	2	–	–	2	–	2	1	6	19
										TOTAL			377	181

APPENDIX B—MATCH APPEARANCES

LIONS TOUR 1968 MATCH APPEARANCES	MATCH NUMBER																				TOTALS
	1	2	3	4	5	6	7	8	9	10	11	12	13	14	15	16	17	18	19	20	
T. J. Kiernan	FB	FB	-	-	FB	FB	FB	-	-	FB	FB	-	FB	FB	-	FB	Sub	FB	-	FB	13
R. Hiller	-	-	FB	FB	-	-	-	FB	FB	-	-	FB	-	-	FB	-	FB	-	FB	-	8
W. K. Jones	RW	-	LW	LW	-	LW	-	-	-	LW	-	-	-	-	-	-	LW	-	-	-	6
M. Richards	LW	LW	-	-	LW	-	LW	LW	-	-	-	LW	LW	LW	LW	LW	-	LW	-	LW	11
K. Savage	-	RW	-	-	RW	-	RW	RW	RW	RW	RW	-	RW	-	RW	RW	-	-	-	RW	11
A. J. W. Hinshelwood	-	-	RW	RW	-	RW	-	RW	LW	-	LW	RW	-	RW	RW	-	RW	RW	RW	-	11
T. G. R. Davies	C	C	-	-	-	C	C	-	-	C	-	C	C	-	C	C	-	C	-	-	9
F. P. K. Bresnihan	Sub	C	C	-	C	Sub	C	-	C	C	C	-	C	-	C	-	C	C	C	C	15
J. W. C. Turner	C	-	-	OH	C	-	-	C	-	-	C	-	-	C	OH	C	-	-	OH	C	10
W. H. Raybould	-	-	C	C	-	-	-	C	C	-	-	C	-	-	OH	-	-	-	C	-	7
K. S. Jarrett	-	-	-	C	-	C	-	-	-	-	-	-	-	C	-	-	C	-	LW	-	5
C. M. H. Gibson	OH	-	-	-	-	OH	Sub	OH	OH	OH	OH	OH	OH	OH	-	OH	OH	OH	-	OH	14
B. John	-	OH	OH	-	OH	-	OH	-	-	-	-	-	-	-	-		-	-	-	-	4
G. Edwards	IH	-	-	-	IH	IH	IH	-	IH	-	IH	-	-	IH	IH	-	-	-	-	-	8
R. M. Young	-	IH	IH	IH	-	-	-	IH	-	IH	-	IH	IH	-	-	IH	IH	-	-	-	9
G. C. Connell	-	-	-	-	-	-	-	-	-	-	-	-	-	-	-	-	-	IH	IH	IH	3

Lions Tour 1968 Match Appearances	\multicolumn{21}{c}{Match Number}																				
	1	2	3	4	5	6	7	8	9	10	11	12	13	14	15	16	17	18	19	20	Totals
J. Young	H	–	H	–	–	H	H	H	–	–	–	H	–	H	–	–	H	–	H	–	9
J. Pullin	–	H	–	H	H	–	–	–	H	H	H	–	H	–	H	H	–	H	–	H	11
M. J. Coulman	LP	–	TH	LH	–	LH	–	LH	LH	–	–	LH	LH	LH	–	LH	–	–	–	–	10
A. L. Horton	TP	TP	–	–	TP	–	–	TP	–	TP	TP	–	–	TP	TP	TH	–	TH	LH	LH	12
S. Millar	–	LP	LP	–	LP	–	LP	–	–	LP	LP	–	–	–	LH	–	LH	LH	–	–	9
J. P. O'Shea	–	–	–	TH	–	TH	TH	–	TH	–	–	TH	TH	–	–	–	TH	–	TH	–	8
W. J. McBride	L	L	–	–	–	–	L	–	–	–	L	–	–	L	L	L	L	–	–	L	11
W. D. Thomas	L	–	L	L	L	L	–	–	L	L	–	L	–	L	–	Sub	–	L	L	TH	12
P. K. Stagg	–	L	–	L	L	L	L	L	L	L	L	L	L	–	L	L	L	L	L	L	11
P. J. Larter	–	–	L	L	–	–	–	L	L	L	L	–	L	8	8	–	8	–	L	–	12
J. W. Telfer	8	8	–	–	–	–	–	8	8	8	8	–	8	–	–	8	8	8	8	8	11
R. B. Taylor	F	F	8	F	–	8	8	F	–	F	F	F	F	F	F	F	–	–	–	F	14
J. Taylor	–	–	–	–	–	–	–	F	–	–	–	–	–	F	F	–	F	–	F	–	5
M. G. Doyle	F	–	F	F	F	F	F	–	F	F	–	F	–	–	–	–	F	F	F	–	11
R. J. Arneil	–	F	F	–	F	F	F	–	F	–	F	–	F	–	F	F	F	F	–	F	12
K. Goodall	–	–	–	–	–	–	–	–	–	–	–	8	–	Total 1	West	–	–	–	–	–	2

APPENDIX C—POINTS SCORERS

LIONS TOUR 1968 POINTS SCORERS	1	2	3	4	5	6	7	8	9	10	11	12	13	14	15	16	17	18	19	20	TOTAL	
T. J. Kiernan	2P 1C	2C			1C 1P	2C 1P	5P 1C			1P	2PG		4P 2C	1PG		2PG		1P		2PG	84	22PG 9C
R. Hiller			3C 2P	3P 1C 1T				2P 2C	2P 1C 1T			5C 1P			1P 1C		5P 2DG 1C		5C 2P		104	18PG 19C 2T 2DG
W. K. Jones			1T																		3	1T
M. Richards		1T			1T				1T			1T						1T			18	6T
K. Savage		1T													1T						6	2T
A. J. W. Hinshelwood			2T	1T		1T		1T											1T		18	6T
T. G. R. Davies	1T											1T			1T						9	3T
F. P. K. Bresnihan					1T														1T		6	2T
J. W. C. Turner	1T			2DG	1T			1T													15	3T 2DG
W. H. Raybould									1T										1T		6	2T
K. S. Jarrett						2C 1P 1T								1C					1T 1P		18	3C 2P 2T
C. M. H. Gibson						1DG		1T		1T		1T 2DG					1T	1DG			24	4T 4DG
B. John																						
G. Edwards					1T				2T					2T	1T						18	6T
R. M. Young								1T				1T									6	2T

APPENDIX C—POINTS SCORERS

LIONS TOUR 1968 POINTS SCORERS	1	2	3	4	5	6	7	8	9	10	11	12	13	14	15	16	17	18	19	20	TOTAL	
G. C. Connell	–	–	–	–	–	–	–	–	–	–	–	–	–	–	–	–	–	–	–	–	–	–
J. Young	–	–	–	–	–	–	–	–	–	–	–	–	–	–	–	–	–	–	–	–	–	–
J. Pullin	–	–	–	–	–	–	–	–	–	–	–	–	–	–	–	–	–	–	–	–	–	–
M. J. Coulman	–	–	–	–	–	–	–	–	–	–	–	–	1T	–	–	–	–	–	–	–	3	1T
A. L. Horton	–	–	–	–	–	–	–	–	–	–	–	–	–	–	–	–	–	–	–	–	–	–
S. Millar	–	–	–	–	–	–	–	–	–	–	–	–	–	–	–	–	–	–	–	–	–	–
J. P. O'Shea	–	–	–	–	–	2T	–	–	–	–	–	–	–	–	–	–	–	–	–	–	6	2T
W. J. McBride	–	–	–	–	–	–	1T	–	–	–	–	–	–	–	–	–	–	–	–	–	3	1T
W. D. Thomas	–	–	–	–	–	1T	–	–	–	–	–	–	–	–	–	–	–	–	1T	–	6	2T
P. K. Stagg	–	–	–	–	–	–	–	–	–	–	–	–	–	–	–	–	–	–	–	–	–	–
P. J. Larter	–	–	–	–	–	–	–	–	–	–	–	–	–	–	–	–	–	–	–	–	–	–
J. W. Telfer	2T	–	–	–	–	–	–	1T	–	–	–	–	–	–	–	–	–	–	–	–	9	3T
R. B. Taylor	–	–	1T	–	–	–	–	–	–	–	–	1T	–	–	–	–	–	–	–	–	6	2T
J. Taylor	–	–	–	–	–	–	–	–	–	–	–	–	–	–	–	–	–	–	1T	–	3	1T
M. G. Doyle	–	–	–	–	–	–	–	–	–	–	–	1T	–	–	–	–	–	–	1T	–	6	2T
R. J. Arneil	–	–	–	–	–	–	–	–	–	–	–	–	–	–	–	–	–	–	–	–	–	–
K. G. Goodall	–	–	–	–	–	–	–	–	–	–	–	–	–	–	–	–	–	–	–	–	–	–
B. R. West	–	–	–	–	–	–	–	–	–	–	–	–	–	–	–	–	–	–	–	–	–	–
	20	10	24	23	17	32	20	25	23	6	6	37	22	11	14	6	26	9	40	6	377	

MATCH No.	LIONS TOUR 1968 APPENDIX D—INJURIES
1	Gibson – ankle ligaments. Edwards – hamstring. Turner – mouth.
2	Telfer – knee ligaments. J. Taylor – knee ligaments. Davies – achilles tendon.
3	Thomas – Bruised toe.
4	R. Young – groin. R. Taylor – bruised thigh.
5	Pullin – torn tendon on shoulder.
6	Jones – hamstring. Jarrett – bruised shoulder.
7	John – broken collar bone. J. Young – injured back. McBride – cut leg.
8	Taylor – bruised shoulder.
9	Raybould – cut chin. Arneil – cut head.
10	—
11	—
12	O'Shea sent off. Goodall – broken bones in hand.
13	Telfer – damaged knee. Stitches in head.
14	Turner – bruised knee.
15	Edwards – torn hamstring.
16	Coulman – torn ankle ligaments.
17	R. Young – two ribs broken.
18	Davies – dislocated elbow.
19	—
20	—